PLEASING THE COURT

PLEASING THE COURT
Writing Ethical and Effective Briefs

Judith D. Fischer

CAROLINA ACADEMIC PRESS

Durham, North Carolina

Portions of this book appeared previously in the following law review articles:

Bareheaded and Barefaced Counsel: Courts React to Unprofessionalism in Lawyers' Papers, 31 Suffolk U. L. Rev. 1 (1997), and
The Role of Ethics in Legal Writing: The Forensic Embroiderer, the Minimalist Wizard, and Other Stories, 9 Scribes J. Legal Writing 77 (2003–2004).

Library of Congress Cataloging-in-Publication Data

Fischer, Judith D.
    Pleasing the court: writing ethical and effective briefs / by Judith D. Fischer.
        p.   cm.
    Includes bibliographical references.
    ISBN 1-59460-045-7
    1. Legal composition. 2. Briefs. 3. Law—United States—Language.
I. Title.

KF250.F53 2004
808'.06634—dc22   2004007864

CAROLINA ACADEMIC PRESS
700 Kent Street
Durham, NC 27701
Telephone (919) 489-7486
Fax (919) 493-5668
www.cap-press.com

Printed in the United States of America

for my teachers, Ruth Durbin Fischer, Sister Anicetus, O.P.,
and Dr. Warren Dwyer
my mentor, Joseph A. Ball
and
John, Niki, Polly, Carrie, Neil, and Andrew
who make it all worthwhile

CONTENTS

Introduction   ix

Chapter 1   State the Law Accurately   1

Chapter 2   State the Facts Accurately   15

Chapter 3   Provide Cogent Analysis   19

Chapter 4   Write Clearly   23

Chapter 5   Avoid Wordiness and Legalese   27

Chapter 6   Avoid Grammar, Spelling, Punctuation,
             and Typographical Errors   33

Chapter 7   Cite Correctly   39

Chapter 8   Follow Court Rules   41

Chapter 9   Do Not Plagiarize   49

Chapter 10   Be Civil   53

Appendix   Guidelines and Exercises   57
             State the Law Accurately (Chapter 1)   57
             State the Facts Accurately (Chapter 2)   60
             Provide Cogent Analysis (Chapter 3)   61
             Write Clearly, Avoiding Wordiness
                 and Legalese (Chapters 4–5)   64
             Avoid Grammar, Spelling, Punctuation, and
             Typographical Errors (Chapter 6)   75

Cite Correctly (Chapter 7)   84
Follow Court Rules (Chapter 8)   87
Do Not Plagiarize (Chapter 9)   88
Be Civil (Chapter 10)   91

Table of Cases Cited   93

Index   101

INTRODUCTION

A story survives about an advocate in Elizabethan England who filed a long, wordy brief.[1] The court showed its displeasure by ordering the brief to be hung, written side outward, around his neck. He was then paraded "bareheaded and barefaced round about Westminster Hall, whilst the Courts [were] sitting...." This incident recently stirred a judge's "nostalgia for the rigors of the common law" as he struggled through a wordy brief.[2] As today's judges decry wordiness and other errors in legal documents and politicians call for curbs on frivolous court filings, this tale of the bareheaded lawyer provides today's legal writers with a vivid image of what not to do.

All agree that whether it is incisive or inept, lawyers' writing affects clients, opposing parties, the courts, and the legal system. When a lawyer fails to inform the court of relevant adverse authority, the court must spend valuable time and effort performing its own analysis. Worse, it may miss the chance to evaluate another court's reasoning and thus formulate a consistent decision. Another error—misrepresenting facts—requires courts to spend time checking sources and may even lead to an unjust decision. Even poor writing style requires judges to waste time deciphering it, a task that prompted one court to exhort counsel "not to clog the system" with unclear briefs. *N/S Corp. v. Liberty Mut. Ins. Co.* Violations of court rules also harm the system, because the rules promote orderly arguments that lead to sound decisions. All of these lapses are unprofessional, because they fail to meet the legal profession's standards of competence and public service.

---

1. Mylward v. Weldon (1596), *in* 1 George Spence, The Equitable Jurisdiction of the Court of Chancery 376-77 n.*h* (1846).

2. Varda, Inc. v. Ins. Co. of N. Am., 45 F.3d 634, 641 (2d Cir. 1995) (citing *Mylward, in* Spence, *supra* note 1, at 377).

What happens to lawyers who submit unprofessional writing to the courts? While no lawyer has recently been ordered to parade around wearing a wordy brief, judges continue to find a variety of ways to express displeasure at unprofessional writing. This book examines the characteristics of good legal writing by presenting courts' reactions to a spectrum of lawyers' lapses, ranging from misrepresentations of the law to verbosity and typographical errors. The courts' reactions are classified by type of error and, within types, by court reactions ranging from bar discipline to stern judicial comments. The focus is on errors that occur in the research and writing process, not those that pervade a lawyer's approach and only incidentally manifest themselves in the written word, because those problems receive adequate treatment elsewhere. Exercises in the Appendix provide practice at avoiding the errors discussed in the text.

The cases examined here may interest lawyers and law students seeking guidance on how to write well. They may also interest those concerned about the health of our legal system. For while these cases record lawyers' errors, they also show that the system encourages high ethics and professionalism. Lawyers who write unprofessional documents may incur bar discipline or financial loss. They also risk losing credibility with the very judges who rule on their cases.

Lest this book create an inaccurately negative impression of lawyers, I want to emphasize that many lawyers write documents of high professional quality. Busy courts sometimes take the trouble to point this out. One judge, for example, "express[ed] appreciation to counsel" for briefs that were "models of clarity and precision, and evidence[d] prodigious labors." *Ray v. Chisum.* Other judges have commended counsel for "well written briefs, superior arguments, and... exemplary courtesy and professionalism," *Quirk v. Premium Homes, Inc.,* and "well written, dispassionate, informative" briefs, In re *Estate of Kendall.* But it is lawyers' errors that I focus on here to provide helpful cautionary examples for law students and lawyers who want to sharpen their writing skills.

Judith D. Fischer
Associate Professor of Law
Louis D. Brandeis School of Law
University of Louisville

PLEASING THE COURT

CHAPTER 1

STATE THE LAW ACCURATELY

Stating the law accurately is the very essence of lawyering. As one court explained, "An empty head but a pure heart is no defense" when a lawyer misstates the law. *Thornton v. Wahl.* Lawyers have a common-law duty to their clients to familiarize themselves with the law and provide competent representation. This duty is reinforced by the American Bar Association's Model Rules of Professional Conduct,[1] now adopted in many states, which provide that a lawyer must competently represent a client. Lawyers have a related ethical duty not to bring claims without adequate legal grounding, a duty that is codified in Federal Rule of Civil Procedure 11 and in 28 U.S.C. § 1927. Many state statutes also permit courts to fine lawyers and even clients who bring unfounded claims.

When a lawyer fails to state the law accurately, it may not be clear whether the misstatement was intentional or negligent. Courts are often reluctant to label attorneys' misstatements deliberate, but they leave no doubt that deliberate deception is a serious matter. One court was "deeply troubled" that a lawyer cited a general rule but failed to mention its exception. *Northwestern Nat'l Ins. Co. v. Guthrie.* While grudgingly assuming that this omission was not intentional but the result of "sloppy research and writing," the court called the lawyer's conduct "perilously close to a violation of the legal profession's ethical canons." Another court said it was "unable to discern whether sloppy research or warped advocacy tactics" led a lawyer to omit an important case and cite an overruled one, but it admonished the lawyer that "diligent research," which includes using Shepard's to update cases, "is

---

1. *See* Model Rules of Prof'l Conduct R. 1.1 (1995).

a professional responsibility." *Cimino v. Yale Univ.* A third court said lawyers "would be guilty of gross incompetence" if they "discovered but intentionally failed to disclose.... an obviously controlling case." *Glassalum Eng'g Corp. v. 392208 Ontario Ltd.*

Other errors appear to be not intentional but negligent and may be caused by poor research or failure to correctly analyze authorities. Courts do not always resolve the questions of intent and underlying cause when addressing misrepresentations of the law. But they may punish the behavior in a variety of ways, as the cases in this chapter illustrate.

Avoid Misstating the Law

Intentional or Reckless Misstatements

Intentional and reckless misstatements of the law can be so egregious as to merit bar discipline. In In re *Shepperson*, a lawyer had submitted briefs that, among other errors, both omitted relevant legal authority and misrepresented cases he did cite. Taken together, his errors caused the Vermont Board of Professional Conduct to conclude that the briefs did not meet "the minimum standard for brief-writing" required of practicing lawyers and that the lawyer did not give "appropriate attention" to his work. He was suspended until he could demonstrate his fitness to practice law. And when another lawyer filed several documents that violated rules of the bankruptcy court, he was publicly reprimanded in a disciplinary proceeding and ordered to take courses in legal writing and bankruptcy law. In re *Hawkins*.

In another case, the discipline took the form of a citation for contempt. *Hi-Tek Bags, Ltd., v. Bobtron Int'l.* There, a plaintiff's lawyer had improperly disclosed information protected by court order. When the defendants moved for sanctions, the plaintiff's lawyer, among other transgressions, misstated the law. This further inflamed the judge's ire, leading to the contempt citation and dismissal of the plaintiff's claims.

Other misstatements result in sanctions. The Seventh Circuit upheld Rule 11 sanctions against a corporation in the amount of $7,025 for frivolous arguments based on "deliberate mischaracterization of precedent," cautioning that "Rule 11 requires at a minimum that a party… school itself in principles of the law that directly apply to the arguments at hand." *Teamsters Local No. 579 v. B & M Transit, Inc.* The same circuit sanctioned another lawyer for reckless misstatements.

In an acrimonious divorce case, where the wife's counsel made a "preposterous" misstatement of law without citing authority, the Seventh Circuit required the wife and her lawyer to pay "double [the husband's] costs and the reasonable attorneys' fees" under Rule 11. *Thornton v. Wahl.* The court reproached counsel: "An empty head but a pure heart is no defense" for misstating the law.

Failure to shepardize resulted in $1,500 sanctions for costs and attorneys' fees when a lawyer doggedly relied on a vacated opinion. *Smith v. United Transp. Union Local No. 81.* His failure to "favor the court with a citation" to the newer opinion was more than mere sloppiness, the court said, because he had "remained unrepentant" even after opposing counsel provided the citation.

Doctoring quoted material can amount to a misrepresentation of the law, as happened in *Precision Specialty Metals, Inc., v. United States.* That case turned on whether a lawyer had filed certain papers "forthwith." She quoted a case's definition of "forthwith" that would have encompassed the 12-day period she took to file the papers, but she omitted the case's next sentence, which added the important qualification that "forthwith" usually means "within 24 hours." The court formally reprimanded her for attempting to mislead it about the content of the precedent case.

One judge took a more creative approach, ordering a lawyer to bring her superior to court to talk about "the overall poor quality of [her] brief." Calling her explanation of a precedent case "dead wrong," the judge found it either "extremely sloppy" or "intentionally misleading" and ordered the lawyer to show cause why she should not be sanctioned under Rule 11. *Hernandez v. N.Y. Law Dept. Corp. Counsel.*

Yet other misstatements of the law bring judicial reproaches. A stinging criticism in a dissent was the final outcome in *Golden Eagle Distributing Corp. v. Burroughs Corp.* (1984), a case where Rule 11 sanctions were reversed. That court confronted the tension between lawyers' dual duties of vigorous advocacy and candor with the court.

A lawyer had made a creative argument on dubious grounds in a motion for summary judgment without labeling it as an argument for "extension, modification, or reversal of existing law." The district court required him to pay the other side's attorneys' fees on the ground that the argument should have been so labeled. But the Ninth Circuit reversed, reasoning that such a labeling requirement would be detrimental to advocacy and the interests of the court. When the court denied an en banc hearing, five Ninth Circuit judges delivered a caustic dissent sympathetic to a trial judge who had finally said "'Enough.'" *Golden Eagle Distrib. Corp. v. Burroughs Corp.* (1987). Attributing less good faith to the lawyers than did the majority, the dissenters denounced the offending brief because it "flatly misrepresented Minnesota law," "insinuated that federal law on the same issue was definitively established the way the defendant would have liked," and "set out California law without qualification and without mention of later authority which for purposes of the present opinion is assumed to have been 'directly contrary.'"

Another group of attorneys received a stern warning for misrepresenting a precedent case. *Bruther v. Gen. Elec. Co.* Their motion papers said the identity of a certain tire was not at issue in the case. The court was therefore "shocked" to read the opinion and learn that the tire's identity *was* at issue. Finding the lawyers' explanation of the case "imprecise, if not outright deceptive," the court decried their "sloppy lawyering" and warned them to "tread lightly for you have exhausted the Court's patience."

Negligent Misstatements

Some lawyers' misstatements of the law are not intentional but occur because they lack knowledge of the relevant law. "There is nothing strategic or tactical about ignorance," as a court once explained in upholding a severe consequence against a lawyer. *Smith v. Lewis.* He had failed to conduct adequate research in a divorce case and therefore did not assert his client's community property interest in her husband's retirement benefits. When she sued for malpractice, the jury found the lawyer's conduct negligent and awarded $100,000 in damages. The lawyer appealed, contending that the law had been unsettled at the time he gave his advice. However, the California Supreme Court said the major reference works at the time uniformly indicated that pension benefits were generally community property. Although California courts had not finally foreclosed all conflicts on the issue, "no significant authority" proposed a contrary result. The court then emphasized the lawyer's duty to know well-settled principles of law and to discover other rules "which, although not commonly known, may readily be found by standard research techniques." While the court recognized that lawyers must make tactical decisions in litigation, it pointed out that a lawyer who fails to perform adequate research deprives the client of the informed judgment to which the client is entitled. The court called the lawyer's conduct culpable and upheld the malpractice judgment.

In another malpractice case, *Baird v. Pace*, a statute prescribed the procedure for perfecting a security interest in a liquor license. But attorney Pace, who represented the holder of a security interest, did no research to find out how to perfect the client's interest. Instead he relied mainly on other lawyers in his office. He did not file the proper documents, the security interest was not perfected, and his client sued him for malpractice. A judgment against the attorney was affirmed on appeal, with the court noting that the error was due to failure to conduct necessary research.

Liability for abuse of process is another possible consequence of failure to state the law accurately. In *Taylor v. Belger Cartage Service, Inc.,* the defendants in the underlying case filed motions for summary judgment. In opposing the motions, the plaintiff's lawyer did "virtually no legal research." Believing that his principal authority was good law, he did not shepardize it, although shepardizing would have disclosed that the case had been limited to its facts. The judge castigated the lawyer for not finding "the easily ascertainable and clear legal standard" that applied to the case. As in *Smith v. Lewis,* the judge recognized that lawyers must be free to make tactical decisions. But he emphasized that lawyers must analyze the law and facts before "subjecting a person or company to the disruption of defending a lawsuit." Quoting Nineteenth Century lawyer Elihu Root, the judge added, "About half of the practice of a decent lawyer is telling would-be clients that they are damned fools and should stop." He held the lawyer liable for abuse of process and ordered him to pay the defendant's attorney's fees.

Case dismissal was just one of the consequences for a lawyer who did not know a basic requirement of the civil rights claim she pleaded. *Clement v. Pub. Serv. Elec. & Gas Co.* Part of her excuse for misunderstanding the law was that the annotated code for the relevant statute was several hundred pages long. The judge found this explanation "simply mind-boggling" and questioned whether the lawyer was "competent to practice law at all." She had also copied her complaint from a form book without performing her own analysis. The combination of these lapses led the judge to dismiss her complaint, propose rule 11 sanctions, and order her to take courses in federal practice and procedure and civil rights law. He also referred the matter to the state ethics office. Another lawyer incurred dismissal and a stern reprimand for filing a brief replete with errors, including citing a depublished case in violation of a California rule. *N/S Corp. v. Liberty Mut. Ins. Co.*

A criminal lawyer's work may be found wanting when his convicted client asserts ineffectiveness of counsel in a habeas corpus petition. That's what happened to one lawyer who did not inform his client of his right to a jury trial on a third drunk-driving offense. *McGurk v. Stenberg.* The lawyer was unaware of the controlling case, which had been decided seven months before the trial. The district court saw this as an "unprofessional error[]" but declined to grant the client's petition because it believed no actual prejudice was established. But the Eighth Circuit reversed and remanded the case, holding that the lawyer's assistance was both ineffective and prejudicial.

Faulty research led to sanctions against a plaintiff's lawyer who omitted two controlling cases from his brief. *Schutts v. Bently Nev. Corp.* He tried to exonerate himself by blaming opposing counsel for not citing the cases and by making the "truly bizarre argument" that the circuit court's authority was not controlling in a Nevada federal court until the Supreme Court should resolve a conflict among circuits on the point. The court sanctioned the plaintiff and his lawyer a total of $7,593.69 for "abuses of this court's scant resources," explaining that while it had no wish to deter meritorious claims, "everyone suffers" when lawyers file frivolous papers.

When one group of lawyers cited outdated law, the court issued an order to show cause why Rule 11 sanctions should not be imposed. *Gould v. Kemper Nat'l Ins. Cos.* The court pointed out that "five minutes of research" about a case the lawyers cited would have revealed the problem. The district court's published opinion referred to the lawyers' "sloppiness and inattention" on that score. When they objected to this language, they compounded their earlier errors by failing to mention a fact so relevant that omitting it "border[ed] on misrepresentation." The judge was unimpressed with their concern that the written criticisms would damage their reputation, stating that any such damage was "not, I think, undeserved." He left the criticisms in the opinion and ordered the offending law firm to show cause why it should not be sanctioned under Rule 11 for bringing the motion.

Another lawyer was threatened with sanctions in *Lieber v. ITT Hartford Insurance Center, Inc.* There, Hartford's counsel presented an overruled case as controlling law, and, because he misread a Westlaw entry, erroneously stated that another case had not been cited recently. The court pointed out that a case can still be good law even if it has not been cited recently and remanded the case for a determination of whether Hartford should be required to pay the plaintiff's attorney's fees because it had not fairly evaluated the case.

Other failures to state the law correctly have evoked strong judicial comments. When counsel misrepresented the holdings of three different cases, a judge reproved them for engaging in "a disturbing pattern: the repeated citation of authority in an inappropriate, out of context manner." *Wallace Computers Servs. v. David Noyes & Co.* Although the judge was uncertain whether the misrepresentations were intentional or due to failure to read beyond favorable language, he found the lawyers' conduct "unacceptable." The lawyers attempted to justify their conduct and asked the court to remove its strong language from its opinion. The judge retained the critical language and delivered a lecture about the ill effects of misrepresenting the law:

> The Northern District of Illinois… is sorely pressed for time and resources. Our job is only made all the more difficult when attorneys use authority out of context or in an otherwise questionable manner, a practice that not only slows

down our efforts, but also serves to reduce our faith in the papers before us.

Provide Sufficient Legal Authority

Minimalist analytic wizardry may have a place in a coffee-shop discussion, but it is inappropriate in the practice of law. *See Bradshaw v. Unity Marine Corp.* When writing to a court, a lawyer must support arguments with appropriate legal authority. Lawyers who failed to do so have incurred sanctions, dismissals, and strong rebukes.

One lawyer's failure to present relevant authority misled her emotionally vulnerable clients, former United States hostages in Iran. *Roeder v. Islamic Republic of Iran.* In their suit against the Republic of Iran, their lawyer failed to provide supporting authority and omitted important opposing authority. Holding her arguments meritless, the court declared that "[a]n attorney cannot carry out the practice of law like an ostrich with her head in the sand, ignoring her duty to research and acknowledge adverse precedent." The poor briefing was especially troubling to the judge because of the emotional toll the case took on the former hostages. In dismissing the case, he expressed regret at disappointing the plaintiffs' hopes but asked "how high those hopes were raised in the first place and on whose shoulders that responsibility should fall."

Another lawyer failed to provide required citations to authority and omitted a major issue. *Chapman v. Hootman.* The court required his client to pay the opposing party $5,000 for fees and expenses for the appeal, declaring that "[t]here is no room at the courthouse for frivolous litigation," which burdens the opposing party, the courts, and legitimate litigants.

Some courts simply refuse to consider unsupported points. For example, when one group of lawyers submitted "naked assertions that are rarely clothed with citation to the record or to pertinent authority," the court declined to consider the unsupported arguments. *Avery v. State Farm Mut. Auto. Ins. Co.* Another lawyer filed a criminal appeal that failed to identify the standard of review and cited only one statute and one case. *Walder v. State.* Because of this lack of appropriate authority, the court called the brief inadequate and ordered the lawyer to file a satisfactory brief or be referred for disciplinary action. When other lawyers failed to provide adequate support for their arguments, Judge Samuel B. Kent called their work "minimalist analytical wizardry." *Bradshaw v. Unity Marine Corp.* He described a defendant's motion as "bumbling" because it was supported by only one irrelevant authority. The plaintiff's opposing memorandum fared no better: its "equally gossamer wisp of an argument" cited an irrelevant case with an erroneous volume number and no pinpoint cite. Explaining that he had received "no useful guidance whatever from either party" because of their lawyers' "heroic efforts to obscure" the issue, the judge sarcastically urged the lawyers to use pencil instead of crayon when writing their next briefs. Judge Kent is noted for his impatience with lawyers, and some have found his tone and comments too harsh, but fair or not, the *Bradshaw* opinion is another illustration of what can befall the careless legal writer.

Disclose Relevant Case Law

Although courts rely on lawyers to cite the major controlling authorities, some lawyers are tempted to use the "ostrich-like tactic" of omitting unfavorable citations. *Borowski v. DePuy, Inc.* Several lawyers who tried that tactic have been sanctioned or rebuked.

Sometimes such omissions are intentional or reckless. The Seventh Circuit upheld sanctions against a lawyer and his client in the amount of costs and attorneys' fees because they "pretend[ed] that potentially dispositive authority against [their] contention [did] not exist." *Borowski v. DePuy, Inc.* Sanctions also resulted when an attorney tried to deflect a court's attention from a relevant case. *Griffith v. Hess Oil V.I. Corp.* While a motion was pending, another judge in the same court issued an opinion on parallel facts. When the plaintiffs' counsel wrote to inform the court of the new opinion, the defendant's lawyer moved to strike the letter as an "unauthorized communication" because the plaintiffs' counsel had not received permission to file an additional pleading as required by a local rule. The court pointed out that its rules require counsel to inform the court of relevant law, and found the motion to strike a "conscious and deliberate effort... to withhold highly relevant case authority from the court" and "the antithesis of an attorney's ethical duty." Because of this bad faith, the court under its inherent power required the defendant's attorney to personally pay the plaintiffs $500 in sanctions.

Some failures to cite relevant authority arise from lawyers' inadequate knowledge of the law. One group of lawyers, for example, failed to cite a case that limited their claim. *Pierotti v. Torian.* In an appeal of an arbitration award, defendant Torian's attorneys omitted a controlling case that established an "extremely limited scope of review of arbitration decisions." Besides omitting this key case, the defendant's brief contained numerous other errors: it lacked required citations to the record, quoted documents not part of the record, and repeated unsupported assertions even after opposing counsel pointed them out. The court required Torian and his counsel to pay the plaintiff $26,000 in costs in addition to the attorney's fees allowed under the parties' contract. But the court did not stop there. Explaining that the behavior of Torian and his lawyers had damaged not only the defendant but also the appellate system, waiting litigants, and the taxpayers, the court added $6,000 in sanctions payable to the court and ordered that its opinion be sent to the State Bar.

Apparently it was forgetfulness that led to sanctions against another lawyer who omitted a precedent case in which he himself had been the attorney. *Tyler v. State.* He said he had remembered the facts of the pending case incorrectly and therefore thought the precedent case did not apply. The court pointed out that the requirement of citations to the record should guard against flawed memories and that the lack of needed citations showed the lawyer had not reviewed parts of the record before he wrote his brief. The court then reminded him that ethical rules require lawyers to cite directly adverse authority that the judge would reasonably consider important. Adding that a lawyer who fails to identify contrary authority cannot correctly advise the client about whether to pursue an appeal, the court fined the lawyer, but limited the amount to $250 because he might not have acted in bad faith.

A similar problem arose in *Massey v. Prince George's County,* where a county attorney's office failed to cite a relevant case in which the county had been a party. Counsel for Prince George's County stated the wrong standard for determining excessive force by the police, but did not mention the "directly adverse" case. Based on the county's misleading papers, the court granted its summary judgment motion. When the court later learned of the controlling case, it ordered the county to show cause why the case had not been cited, emphasizing counsel's duty "to provide 'competent representation,' which includes an ability to research the law." Noting that cases are available both in books and on line, the court observed that Westlaw's Natural Language search would have disclosed the controlling case. The court was especially disturbed because the county had been the defendant in the precedent case it failed to cite. Still, believing that the attorney assigned to the case did not actually know of the precedent, the court declined to impose sanctions. But it did order the county attorney's office to provide a list of all similar cases against it where dispositive motions had been filed after a certain date. The judge then wrote to the judges in those cases to advise them of the pending proceeding and of the county's failure to cite the controlling case.

Another judge bluntly stated that adopting a lawyer's arguments would have caused him to apply the law incorrectly. *Prickett v. DeKalb County.* He was "quite troubled" by the lawyer's "loose interpretation of the law" and failure to cite controlling contrary authority. Another judge chastised both counsel for a variety of errors. *Jordan v. Reis.* Neither side cited major cases that were directly on point. The lawyers also omitted important facts, and the plaintiff's papers were "incoherent at many junctures," partly because "haphazardly placed" correction fluid "render[ed] the 'doctored' sentences incomprehensible." The judge reproached both lawyers for their "seriously inadequate briefing."

Update the Law

Some mistakes about the law occur because a lawyer simply fails to update authority. An old malpractice case forewarns those who make this mistake. *Estate of A.B.* A deceased lawyer had failed to check for new statutes, and as a result he gave his client erroneous advice. Emphasizing the lawyer's professional duty to know the law, the court held his estate liable for the client's damages, adding that perhaps the lawyer "had forgotten the saying that 'no man's life, liberty or property are safe while the legislature is in session.'"

More recently, failure to update authority prompted a court to lay a humbling requirement on a lawyer. *Salahuddin v. Coughlin.* The court could "not fathom" how he omitted references to controlling cases that would be found if he shepardized cases he did cite. The court ordered him to show cause why he should not be sanctioned and required him to submit all further papers with a senior attorney's affidavit of approval.

Another lawyer's reliance on an outdated case initially led the court to an erroneous view of the law. *Doering v. Pontarelli Builders, Inc.* Upon discovering the newer authority, the court reproached the lawyer in print: "A party not only fails to benefit but loses the court's trust when it fails to disclose contradictory precedent." Similarly, in *DeMyrick v. Guest Quarters Suite Hotels,* the court found it "particularly distressing" that a lawyer cited outdated authority because of apparent failure to update the case through Shepard's or computer sources. And the same judge chastised another lawyer for citing an off-point case and relying on an "expressly overruled" one: the judge remarked that it is "really inexcusable" to cite a case without shepardizing or updating it on line. *Gosnell v. Rentokil, Inc.*

The cliche about minding one's P's and Q's took on new meaning when one lawyer appealed the dismissal of his case. *Glassalum Eng'g Corp. v. 392208 Ontario Ltd.* On the motion in the trial court, neither side cited the governing case, an omission that led to the erroneous dismissal. Had the lawyers shepardized a case they did cite, they would have found the notation "q," signifying that the cited case had been questioned, undermining its force as good law. The appellate court reinstated the pending case, lecturing counsel, "We are distressed that neither appellant's counsel nor appellee's counsel favored us or the trial court with citation to any of the cases referred to in our opinion, which are completely dispositive of the issue presented." The court then reminded the bar that lawyers must update cases, "mind[ing] the 'p's' and 'q's'" when they do so.

Two other lawyers apparently failed to delve behind "overruled" notations in Shepard's. *Lewis v. Paul Revere Life Ins. Co.* The court reproached both lawyers for arguing that cases had been overruled, although they were overruled on grounds not relevant to the pending issues.

Cite Only Relevant Sources

Judges sometimes find it necessary to explain that certain sources carry little weight in a court of law. One lawyer cited only the New Testament and Bob Dylan, thus providing no cognizable authority for the novel notion that a state's appellate court could overrule its highest court. Finding her argument "unfathomable," the court dismissed her case. *Commonwealth v. Dube.* Another court reminded counsel that citations to legal encyclopedias are not adequate legal authority and declined to consider the arguments so advanced. *Randall v. Salvation Army.* Elsewhere, a dissenting justice took the majority to task for "conducting an embarrassing google.com search for information outside the record" and for relying on secondary sources like a student comment and a slanted article from the popular press. *People v. Mar.*

Commendations for Good Research

Judges do appreciate good research and sometimes say so. For example, in *Henson v. Thezan,* the court praised the lawyers on both sides: "Not only did they discover [new cases] within days of issuance, but they then incorporated the cases into well-reasoned and well-written briefs on behalf of their clients." And in *Bridwell v. State,* the court commended counsel for informing it about a relevant case that appeared after the opening briefs were filed.

CHAPTER 2

STATE THE FACTS ACCURATELY

Stating the facts accurately is another key element of the lawyer's job. "Creative renditions" of facts breach a lawyer's duty to investigate a case and present its facts accurately. *See N/S Corp. v. Liberty Mut. Ins. Co.* When a lawyer makes inaccurate statements, the court must spend extra time checking for errors. Worse, the inaccuracies may lead to an unjust result.

Misrepresentations of fact may be due to pervasive ethical problems that extend beyond the writing process, as when a lawyer was disbarred after he manufactured a bank sale prospectus to "cure" a problem with a witness's testimony (In re *Richards*), or when another lawyer fabricated a will (In re *Nolan*). Another attorney wrote a false affidavit that rose to the level of "recklessly negligent conduct" and led to his suspension from practice for eighteen months. *Nebraska ex rel. Neb. State Bar Ass'n v. Zakrzewski.* Inaccuracies caused by pervasive ethical problems like these are not the primary focus of this book. Other misrepresentations are tied more closely to the writing process.

Such lapses can lead to disciplinary action. A public reprimand resulted where a lawyer wrote letters impugning a judge's integrity in false statements that were made "at a minimum...with reckless disregard for the truth." *Fla. Bar v. Ray.* Another lawyer was referred to a disciplinary panel after misstating the record on an appeal, an error he had made in the past. *Qualls v. Apfel.* And a court admonished another lawyer for filing brief so full of factual misstatements that it bore "little resemblance to the actual dispute presented to the court." *Nguyen v. IBP, Inc.*

Factual misstatements may also lead to sanctions. One lawyer whose brief "grossly misstated" a case record was ordered to pay $5,000 in sanctions. In re *Guevara*. The court also required him to take a course in advanced civil procedure. Another a lawyer's misrepresentation of the record was called "flagrant" and "thoroughly misleading and unprofessional" and prompted an order that he pay the other side's costs and attorney's fees. *Borowski v. DePuy*. When another lawyer submitted an affidavit that contained "selective and misleading quotations" from a lease, the court ordered him to show cause why he should not be sanctioned. *Copelco Capital, Inc., v. Gen. Consul of Bol.*

Some lawyers' misstatements of fact are due to inadequate investigation. A lawyer who sued a funeral home was sanctioned for falsely representing that his client was the decedent's son, although events should have alerted him to investigate that point. *Stone v. House of Day Funeral Serv., Inc.* Faulty memory and failure to review the record closely were the apparent causes of another lawyer's fine for errors that included misstating facts. *Tyler v. State*.

Inaccurately presenting the facts may also cause a lawyer to lose a case. This happened when one lawyer submitted made-up facts that the Ninth Circuit called "creative renditions of what actually occurred at the district court." *N/S Corp. v. Liberty Mut. Ins. Co.* This obliged the court to look through the record for the alleged information, much of which was "not there at all." Noting that courts have a high volume of work and limited resources, the Ninth Circuit declared, "[w]e must insist that parties not clog the system by presenting us with a slubby mass of words rather than a true brief." Stating that the appellant had "approached our rules with such insouciance that we cannot overlook its heedlessness," the court struck the offending brief and dismissed the appeal.

Another lawyer lost his case because of his misrepresentation of fact. He drafted a deed he knew to be inconsistent with the parties' contract, burying the inconsistency in "an almost incomprehensible, three page single spaced description containing only four sentences." *Cont'l Land Co. v. Inv. Props Co.* Because of this chicanery, the court enforced the sale as stated in the contract and awarded damages to the aggrieved party. Elsewhere, a lawyer opposed to a motion to dismiss by misstating the record in a different but related case. *Clarke v. Brandolini.* The court granted the motion, although it gave the offending lawyer leave to amend. Some factual misstatements simply prompt judges' negative comments. Clerical error may have been the explanation for some of the errors in one brief, although the court pointed out that other errors were "generalizations and overstatements that bordered on deception." *Am. Nat'l Bank & Trust Co. of Chi. v. Harcros Chems., Inc.* For example, the lawyers described a lease by using ellipses in a way that amounted to an "attempt to mislead the court." The court chastised the erring lawyers, warning them that "attention to detail is critical," because "sloppy argument greatly multiplies the proceedings."

CHAPTER 3

PROVIDE COGENT ANALYSIS

Cogent analysis is integral to good legal writing. Arguments that are poorly founded or "vanish in a twinkling" (*see Avery v. State Farm Mut. Auto. Ins. Co.*) lead to substandard documents, as courts have reminded several lawyers.

An attorney's "crimped and skewed view of the controlling cases" was part of the basis for sanctions in one federal case. *United States* ex rel. *Sampson v. Crescent City E.M.S., Inc.* There, the plaintiff's lawyer filed new complaints after a court dismissed related ones on the same facts. The court found the lawyer's persistent pursuit of "copycat" claims "shocking." Moreover, the lawyer's brief in the pending case "present[ed] utterly preposterous arguments" and was a "consummate study [in] how to avoid the real issue." The court assessed sanctions in the amount of attorney's fees and expenses and also ordered the lawyer to reveal the sanction order to any other court where he filed a complaint.

Fees and costs were also assessed against another lawyer who submitted only "vague and directionless sentences" and long block quotations of case law. *Morters v. Barr.* Because the brief lacked any application of law to the facts, the court said the lawyer did not even "set forth an 'argument'" as required by court rule.

It "pained" a court to read another lawyer's analysis that was so "replete with unnecessary, baseless, irrelevant, and frivolous claims" that a layperson could be expected to do better. *Lockheed Martin Energy Sys., Inc., v. Slavin.* Then, on a Rule 11 motion against him, the lawyer repeated his baseless arguments and added personal accusations against the opposing party and its lawyer. This conduct, the court said, showed a "callous disregard for the operation and efficient functioning of the Court." Noting that the lawyer's previous offensive conduct had caused other judges to bar him from their courts, the court formally reprimanded him and ordered him to pay the opposing party's costs and fees and apologize for the personal attacks.

One lawyer's entire appeal was found frivolous because of his faulty reasoning. *Romala Corp. v. United States.* His irrelevant arguments and poor logic avoided the real issue and included false premises and non sequiturs. This "exceed[ed] all permissible bounds of zealous advocacy" and led to sanctions against the lawyer and his client for twice the amount of the appellee's costs. The court pointed out that such briefing harms the opposing party as well as the public, whose taxes are wasted on a frivolous appeal. Stressing that courts are taking stronger stands against frivolous appeals, the court quoted Judge Posner's admonition that "'some members of the bar still do not realize that the judicial attitude toward attorney misconduct has stiffened. They had better realize it.'" (Quoting *Hill v. Norfolk & W. Ry.*)

In another case, an attorney misunderstood the weight of authority and cited a dissenting opinion as controlling. *Bridges v. Robinson.* She also flouted settled summary judgment principles by "improperly present[ing her] own version of the facts in a manner resembling jury argument." Combined with her failure to adequately brief certain issues, this brought her clients $10,000 in sanctions.

Two other lawyers' poor logic recently resulted in sanctions. For one, "irrelevant, illogical" arguments that were "utterly without any good-faith factual basis" warranted sanctions of $3,675 against both him and his client. *Prop. Movers, L.L.C., v. Goodwin.* Illogic was also a problem for a second lawyer, who wrote arguments that "fl[ew] in the teeth of the plain meaning of the statute" and had "utterly no foundation in law or logic." *Abbs v. Principi.* He also made a "flatly false" statement of law and cited irrelevant cases in response to an allegation of frivolity. The court required him to pay appellate costs and issued a stern warning.

Other courts have simply refused to consider illogical arguments. Where a lawyer failed to identify supporting facts and cited irrelevant cases, a court determined that he had waived his contentions on that issue by failing to make a cogent argument. *Sterling v. Alexander.* A different court rebuked a group of lawyers though metaphor, saying that their arguments "appear from nowhere and then vanish in a twinkling, never to be heard of again." *Avery v. State Farm Mut. Auto.*

Ins. Co. The court refused to consider the undeveloped arguments, stressing that a court is entitled to briefs "that are articulate and organized and present cohesive legal argument." When one lawyer rehashed claims that had already been dismissed, a court reproached him for advancing a position that was "no longer tenable." *Balthazar v. Atl. City Med. Ctr.* He was ordered to take courses in federal practice and procedure and professional responsibility, which the court hoped would familiarize him with "the legal principles that have apparently escaped him" throughout the case. Other lawyers have been reproached for their poor reasoning. In a case where both sides presented irrelevant arguments, a court admonished the lawyers that briefs must contain "cohesive legal argument." *People v. Stork.* Another lawyer analyzed the contracts statute of limitations by citing tort cases, prompting the judge to remind him that different statutes of limitations require different analyses. *Lewis v. Paul Revere Life Ins. Co.*

CHAPTER 4

WRITE CLEARLY

"The power of a clear statement is the great power at the bar," said Daniel Webster.[1] Clear writing is also a professional obligation because both clients and the courts rely on the lawyer's writing to clarify the issues.

Instead of fulfilling this obligation, one Kentucky lawyer filed a "virtually incomprehensible" appellate brief that led to dismissal of his appeal. The offending brief was only a page and a half long and "grossly inadequate." *Kentucky Bar Ass'n v. Brown*. In dismissing the appeal, the court characterized the brief as "little more than fifteen unclear and ungrammatical sentences, slapped together as two pages of unedited text with an unintelligible message." When the bar association charged the lawyer with incompetence, his argument that he should not be suspended because he was trustworthy "highlight[ed] his continued inability to grasp the concept of relevance." The Kentucky Supreme Court suspended him from the practice for sixty days and ordered him to pay the costs of the bar action.

Sometimes a lawyer's poor writing brings financial consequences. One lawyer's brief was so unclear that the court could discern its arguments "only through the exertion of great effort." *Catellier v. Depco, Inc.* The brief also included personal attacks, violated court rules on such matters as the content of the statement of the case, page length, and typeface, and failed to provide pinpoint citations. The court therefore assessed attorney's fees against the lawyer personally.

---

1. Quote It Completely! 27 (Eugene C. Gerhart ed., 1998).

Confusing writing also led to sanctions when a defendant insurance company's lawyer used a case's complex facts to "obfuscate, rather than clarify, the issues." *LaGrange Mem'l Hosp. v. St. Paul Ins. Co.* His brief contained numerous errors: it misled the court about the law, relied on overruled cases, omitted required sections, and exceeded the page limit. In requiring the defendant to pay the plaintiff's fees and costs, the court stressed the importance of an orderly argument in helping it to reach a just result.

Another attorney filed an "undecipherable" complaint that included more than twelve factual allegations in one paragraph, subdivided material in an "incomprehensible" manner, and was "redundant, jumbled, and cryptic." *Rubino v. Circuit City Stores, Inc.* Explaining that "[c]oncise and clear pleadings are vital to the administration of justice," the court required the lawyer personally to pay the defendants' fees and costs.

A court recently imposed some creative sanctions on a repeat offender at poor brief writing. The lawyer's first mistake was to submit a 160-page complaint containing "largely meritless allegations" that were "legally and factually nonsensical." *Leuallen v. Borough of Paulsboro.* Partly because the lawyer had ignored previous admonitions, the judge publicly admonished him, fined him $1,000, and ordered him to and write a 20-page summary of his obligations under Rule 11 and to send the court's opinion to his clients. The lawyer then angered a second judge in the same courthouse, who ordered him to take continuing education classes in professionalism and federal practice and procedure. *Mendez v. Draham.* Undaunted, the lawyer filed a new 392-page complaint before the second judge that was "incomprehensible in its immensity" and, despite its length, was "plainly frivolous." That judge admonished the lawyer for substituting " 'mouse clicks' for legal judgment," stating that it is unprofessional for a lawyer to substitute the cut-and-paste word processing function for the research and draftsmanship he should have done. The judge dismissed the complaint and cautioned the lawyer that further unprofessional conduct would result in a referral for disciplinary action, including suspension or disbarment.

Other lawyers' unclear writing has prompted strong criticism. The Eighth Circuit denounced a plea agreement that "drown[ed] in clauses" as a "monument to legalese," partly because of the drafter's use of the "clumsy" and/or expression. *United States v. Taylor.* A state court described a lawyer's eighty-eight-page complaint as a "blunderbuss." *Brehm v. Eisner.* Another court chastised a lawyer for his wordy complaints filled with "incoherent" claims and "illogical" statements. *Bliss v. Rochester City Sch. Dist.* And when a lawyer advanced undeveloped and incoherent arguments, the Seventh Circuit soundly condemned "litigat[ing] through obfuscation," adding, "This method of litigating is unbecoming for a member of the bar of this court." *Joseph P. Caulfield & Assocs., Inc., v. Litho Prods., Inc.*

CHAPTER 5

AVOID WORDINESS
AND LEGALESE

Verbosity is out of vogue in the legal profession. It has been 150 years since Ohio lawyer Timothy Walker wrote a caricature of a lawyer saying "I give you that orange":

> I give you all and singular my estate and interest, right, title, and claim, and advantage of and in that orange, with all its rind, skin, juice, pulp, and pips, and all right and advantage therein, with full power to bite, cut, suck, and otherwise eat the same, or give the same away, as fully and effectually as I, said A B, am now entitled to bite, cut, suck, or otherwise eat the same orange....[1]

Walker concocted this legalese to illustrate the virtues of its opposite, plain English. Early in the twentieth century, the New York Court of Appeals lamented a 117-page brief in a simple case. The court attributed this excess to the advent of stenography, stating that wordy briefs were less prevalent "[w]hen every lawyer wrote his points with a pen." *Stevens v O'Neill*. The movement toward plain English in the law gathered momentum throughout the twentieth century. Today, experts in the field of legal writing generally agree that concise prose both communicates and persuades better than wordy, cluttered legalese. Legal writing expert Bryan Garner's survey of judges showed that they prefer succinct briefs to wordy

---

1. Mark E. Steiner, *Heroes of the Revolution: Henry D. Sedgwick and Timothy Walker*, 3 Scribes J. Legal Writing 43, 49 (1992) (quoting [Timothy Walker], *Miscellaneous: Law Phraseology*, 5 W. L.J. 574, 574 (1848)).

ones.[2] A judge recently made a similar point, writing that "law students have been taught for at least fifty years" to avoid legalese like *to-wit* and *whereas. State v. Eason.*

But despite advances toward clarity and succinctness, popular humor still portrays lawyers as deliberately writing prolix documents, and courts must sometimes remind lawyers that their language should be "short, comprehending much in few words." *Gordon v. Green.* Indeed, today's lawyers face new temptations as computers enable them to assemble large amounts of information quickly, leading some to "substitute volume for logic in an apparent attempt to overwhelm the courts." *Slater v. Gallman.*

One lawyer's wordiness left a court unable to understand the basis for his arguments. In re *Disciplinary Action Against Pinotti.* His prolix pleadings were part of the basis for his ninety-day suspension from the practice of law. The court also ordered him to take courses in legal ethics, civil procedure, and trial procedure.

Wordy filings may also lead to Rule 11 sanctions. "Unnecessarily prolix and repetitive briefs" brought a large sanction in *Yankee Candle Co. v. Bridgewater Candle Co.* There, in response to the defendant's motion for summary judgment, the plaintiffs attempted to support weak claims with "enormous (and often unenlightening) documents," including a 100-page Memorandum of Law and a 114-page response to the defendant's 10-page Statement of Undisputed Facts. The court stated that the clumsy documents "unduly burdened both defendant and this court" and were based on an improper attempt to harm the defendant financially. To deter such conduct in the future, the court assessed over $1,000,000 in fees and costs against the plaintiff.

Another large sanction was assessed against a plaintiff's lawyer who continually submitted wordy documents in support of baseless claims. *Brandt v. Schal Assocs., Inc.* When the defendant moved for sanctions, the plaintiff's lawyer, not yet having learned his lesson, submitted a 158-page responsive brief outlining the factual support for each claim line by line. The Seventh Circuit decried this "windy,

---

2. Bryan A. Garner, *Judges on Briefing: A National Survey,* 8 Scribes J. Legal Writing 1 (2001–2002).

excessive, and voluminous style of practice," and upheld the district judge's award of over $400,000 in sanctions because of both the lack of foundation for the claims and the lawyer's litigating style.

In awarding sanctions, the New York Court of Appeals expounded about the poor quality and wordiness of a lawyer's brief, noting that its arguments wandered in "seemingly endless fashion." *Slater v. Gallman*. An appellant's lawyer had filed a wordy and unfocused 284-page brief that covered numerous irrelevant points at length and only briefly discussed the real issue. He then compounded his error by adding a four-page explanation of why the brief was so long. The court required the appellant to pay the appellee's costs in the matter.

Wordy writing has also caused cases to be dismissed, especially where counsel neglect to take advantage of repeated opportunities to cure deficiencies in a complaint. An attorney granted leave to amend a complaint will sometimes submit a new pleading that nearly duplicates the original. In one such case, the original complaint was "an amorphous, vague, confused structure." *Johnson v. Hunger*. After it was dismissed with leave to amend, the lawyer filed an amended complaint that repeated much of the original one but added still more prolix allegations. The court dismissed the "foggy mixture" with prejudice. Similarly, after a court dismissed a complaint it called a "disaster," the plaintiff's lawyer filed an amended complaint that merely rephrased the "prolix allegations" of the original, leading to a final dismissal of the action. *Clarke v. Brandolini*.

Another lawyer replaced his dismissed wordy complaint with one that was "still extremely verbose and rambling." The court dismissed his case. *Martin v. Hunt*. Then there was the judge who dismissed a complaint that was "a veritable compendium of prolixity," stating that it "approaches the incredible," containing cross-references that required "painstaking re-shuffling of its 36 pages." *Benner v. Phila. Musical Soc'y*. The judge then had to face the "agonizing task" of reading an equally prolix amended complaint, which he dismissed as an "egregious violation," although he reluctantly granted the lawyer leave to amend.

In dismissing a thirty-seven-page second amended complaint, a federal judge advised its authors to edit and shorten their pleading from its confusing "novelized form." When they continued to submit "prolix, confusing" complaints, their case was dismissed. *McHenry v. Renne.* Elsewhere, a district court dismissed counsel's third amended complaint with prejudice. *Arena Land & Inv. Co. v. Petty.* Although the 143 pages of the original complaint had been reduced to 89, it was still too verbose, rambling on for "sixty-four pages before reaching the first claim for relief."

One court dismissed prolix "complaints, amendments, amended amendments, [and] amendments to amended amendments." *Gordon v. Green.* Counsel in five consolidated cases had filed pleadings exceeding 4,000 pages, "occupying 18 volumes, and requiring a hand truck or cart to move." One of the pleadings contained a one-sentence, single-spaced paragraph that filled an entire legal-sized page. Refusing to "struggle through" pleadings it called "gobbledygook" and "gibberish," the court remarked that if every party filed such lengthy documents, trees would be wasted and a new courthouse would be needed to store the documents.

A verbose complaint warranted dismissal and a reproof in another case. *Morgens Waterfall Holdings, L.L.C., v. Donaldson, Lufkin & Jenrette Sec. Corp.* There, counsel filed a 103-page amended complaint that was "a rhetorical exercise in length and forensic embroidery," "hopelessly redundant," and "excessively long-winded." The court dismissed the complaint, suggesting that counsel file one "in concise, direct, simple form and of reasonable length."

Another judge was so displeased when a lawyer filed a prolix, repetitive complaint that he sent him a pleading from a form book to use as an example. *Politico v. Promus Hotels, Inc.* The judge also urged him to study a classic book on writing, Strunk and White's *The Elements of Style.*

Judges have reproached lawyers for wordiness in several other cases, including one where the court called the complaint a "pastiche of prolix invective." *Brehm v. Eisner.* A court explained the importance of concise briefing with a sardonic comment in *United States v. Molina-Tarazon.* The government had moved to file a brief that exceeded the prescribed word limit. The court denied the motion and sent the government lawyer back to edit the document, commenting dryly, "We have every confidence that when the United States Department of Justice applies its formidable resources to the problem, it will come up with a petition...that complies with our rules, yet presents the government's position elegantly and forcefully."

Having been subjected to so many wordy briefs, courts sometimes express their appreciation of succinct ones. One court praised a concise three-page motion as "an excellent example of proper appellate procedure." *Brown v. State.* Courts have also commended lawyers for abandoning losing arguments and wasting "little effort in getting to the heart of the issues," *Capitol Hardware Mfg. Co. v. Natco, Inc.,* and for writing concise briefs, *State v. Swallow; Commonwealth v. Angiulo.*

CHAPTER 6

AVOID GRAMMAR, SPELLING, PUNCTUATION, AND TYPOGRAPHICAL ERRORS

Good legal writing is polished and professional in appearance. By contrast, errors in form detract from both the writing's appearance and its clarity. One court paraphrased Shakespeare to emphasize the bad impression a lawyer's errors made, writing that "all the perfumes of Arabia would not eviscerate the grammatical stench emanating from this indictment." *Henderson v. State.* Errors in form have brought embarrassing consequences for other lawyers as well.

Grammatical Errors

Poor grammar was one of the grounds for a lawyer's suspension from the practice of law in In re *Hawkins.* The Minnesota Supreme Court explained that, even though Hawkins' client had not been harmed, the legal system was affected: "Public confidence in the legal profession is shaken" when lawyers' documents "are so filled with spelling, grammatical, and typographical errors that they are virtually incomprehensible." In suspending another lawyer, the Kentucky Supreme Court listed ungrammatical sentences among his numerous offenses. *Ky. Bar Ass'n v. Brown.* Poor grammar was also among the errors that provoked another court to order a hearing on Rule 11 sanctions against a lawyer. In re *Generes.*

Because grammatical errors detract from clarity, they have also been among the bases for complaints being dismissed. For example, one plaintiff's counsel repeatedly filed documents "with numerous grammatical errors and misstatements." *Styles v. Phila. Elec. Co.* The court dismissed several of the plaintiff's claims, citing lack of subject-verb agreement, as shown by the statement "Defendant...are," and the use of "he" instead of "she." The court concluded that the lawyer had "not taken the appropriate care to avoid errors," and ordered him to show cause why he should not be sanctioned. In another case, a complaint was dismissed because it violated "the most basic requirements of English grammar." *Huang v. Shiu.* Another court dismissed a complaint that contained many errors, including the phrase "jurisdiction is within the trial courts [sic] desecration [sic]." *Gardner v. Investors Diversified Capital, Inc.*

Sometimes the penalty for a lawyer's grammatical errors is an embarrassing comment on the record. For example, one court said a complaint dismissed on other grounds was "almost impenetrable" because of its flaws in grammar, syntax and logic. In re *Marriage of Green.* Elsewhere, a lawyer wrote an indictment that, due to sentence fragments and omitted words, said the breaking and entering had been done not by the defendant but by the stolen merchandise. *Henderson v. State.* Calling the indictment "atrocious," the judge paraphrased Shakespeare to condemn its "grammatical stench." Although the judge affirmed the conviction, he also stressed the desirability of "a literate bar."

Spelling Errors

Spelling errors were part of an overall pattern of incompetence in two bar discipline cases. The District of Columbia Court of Appeals mentioned spelling problems in combination with other errors when it suspended a lawyer from the practice of law. In re *Stone.* And the Minnesota Supreme Court listed misspellings in its litany of errors when it publicly reprimanded a lawyer for violating court rules and writing documents that were generally substandard. In re *Hawkins.* The court also ordered him to update his skills by taking courses, including a writing course.

Other courts have noted spelling errors with disapproval. One brief that contained spelling errors was called "sloppy." *David v. Village of Oak Lawn*. Another court did not explicitly mention a lawyer's spelling errors, but called attention to them by including four in a quotation from the complaint, adding "[sic]" after each spelling error. *Trapp v. Schuyler Constr.*

Punctuation Errors

Punctuation marks, though small, can have weighty consequences. One case turned on the venerable distinction between restrictive and nonrestrictive modifiers. *Mass. Mut'l Life Ins. Co. v. Aritech Corp.* A lender, MassMutual, contended that its borrower, Aritech, owed a prepayment premium for paying off a loan early. The relevant section of the parties' note provided as follows:

> *Option Prepayment with Premium.* At any time or from time to time, [Aritech] may, at its option, upon notice as provided…prepay all or any part…of the principal amount of the Notes upon the concurrent payment of premium equal to the Make Whole Amount if there shall have been a period of at least 20 consecutive trading days during which the last reported sale price for the shares of Common Stock in the principal market for such shares…was at least 140% of the Conversion Price in effect on each of such days.

This sentence is not a model of clarity and could profitably be divided into at least two sentences. But the court had to construe it as written. MassMutual contended that the sentence meant Aritech could prepay with a premium once the stock reached a certain price. Aritech contended that it could always prepay, but that the premium was required only if the stock reached that price. The resolution turned on whether the phrase beginning "upon the concurrent payment of premium" was restrictive or nonrestrictive. The court observed that when modifying language is not set off by commas, it is *restrictive*—that is, it limits the meaning of the element it modifies. By contrast, modifying language set off by commas is nonrestrictive, or only descriptive. Because no comma appeared before the phrase about prepayment, that phrase was restrictive, meaning that the right to prepay was always accompanied by the obligation to pay a premium. Aritech therefore owed a prepayment premium because of the lack of one comma.

Another court denied a motion because it believed a stray comma changed the meaning of a sentence. *People v. Vasquez.* The court said that the "typographical error of placing a comma" before the phrase "upon information and belief" rendered an affidavit hearsay. It therefore required that an additional affidavit be filed before the pending motion could be granted. And in a criminal case, a misplaced period meant the indictment technically did not charge the defendant with the crime, although the court found the indictment legally sufficient. *Henderson v. State.*

A misplaced apostrophe caused problems in a dispute over a settlement offer. *Maffucci v. City of Phila.* The City of Philadelphia presented a settlement offer of $215,000 to three plaintiffs, and two rejected the offer. One line in the offer, however, stated that the amount offered "represents the total liability for any and all of plaintiff's loss...." The third plaintiff, seizing on this use of the singular possessive word *plaintiff's,* proposed to accept the offer and the entire $215,000. The court pointed out that the word *plaintiff's* was indeed a singular possessive form that technically referred to a sole plaintiff. However, in the context of the whole document, which referred to three plaintiffs, the court found that placement of the apostrophe was a typographical error. Therefore, the third plaintiff had no right to accept the offer alone.

Punctuation errors in court documents are usually not outcome determinative, but they often provoke judicial annoyance. Thus, in one case, where portions of the complaint were dismissed on other grounds, the court lectured counsel:

> [C]ounsel uses possessives without apostrophes, leaving the reader to guess whether he intends a singular or plural possessive, etc. Such sloppy pleading and briefing are inexcusable as a matter of courtesy as well as because of their impact on defendants' ability to respond.... [The court] contemplates the possibility that counsel may seek to file an amended com-

plaint to cure the many defects. If he does that, counsel would be advised to ensure that the amended complaint is also readable.

P.M.F. Servs., Inc. v. Grady

Another court delivered an equally irate lecture, this time to a former clerk of the court. *State v. Bridget.* Noting that his brief contained more than fifty examples of mistakes in punctuation, citation, and spelling, the court urged him "to do credit to his former position" by attending to detail and proofreading his briefs. Another court registered its disapproval by reproducing a lawyer's punctuation errors with the notation "[sic]." *Gardner v. Investors Diversified Capital, Inc.* Yet another court pointed out in a footnote that a trust instrument omitted a necessary apostrophe. *Wells Fargo Bank v. Marshall.* In a statement that must have embarrassed the erring lawyer, the court said that it would add the apostrophe, writing the phrase correctly as "trustor's death," rather than reproduce the error and add *sic* for each reference.

Typographical Errors

Courts often view typographical errors as indicators of a lawyer's general lack of competence. Like grammatical and spelling errors, they often occur in combination with other errors. That was the case in *Teague v. Bakker,* where a lawyer's petition for attorney's fees of over one million dollars was denied partly because he did not provide adequate support for the requested amount. The court called the lawyer's inadequate papers "cavalier," partly because of their numerous typographical errors.

Typographical errors were mentioned as part of one lawyer's overall shoddy performance when he was publicly reprimanded. In re *Hawkins.* And another court mentioned "numerous errors of grammar, orthography, and typography" in finding that the brief of a criminal appeals attorney was so haphazardly done that his representation amounted to ineffective assistance of counsel. In re *Banks.*

A court reduced another lawyer's fee because he submitted papers replete with typographical errors. *Devore v. City of Phila.* The lawyer had responded to opposing counsel's criticism of his errors by submitting additional errors, of which the court reproduced some "favorites": "Further, had the Defendants not tired [sic] to paper Plaintiff's counsel to death, some type [sic] would not have occurred. Furthermore, there have been omissions by Defendants, thus they should not case [sic] stones." The lawyer also made the impolitic error of misspelling the judge's first name. Chastising the lawyer for his "complete lack of care in his written product," the judge cut his requested hourly fee for his written work in half.

CHAPTER 7

CITE CORRECTLY

A lawyer's careful attention to citation format produces references that are accurate and easy to follow. On the other hand, "laissez-faire" citations appear unprofessional and hamper the court's work. *See Hurlbert v. Gordon*. Although courts are sometimes forgiving of the occasional small citation error (*e.g., Cal. Fin. Responsibility Co. v. Pierce*), inaccurate references can annoy judges or clerks by requiring them to conduct time-wasting searches for the correct information.

In one disciplinary proceeding, for example, a lawyer was urged to obtain tutoring in "proper citation form." *In re Shepperson*. He did not do so, and was finally suspended from the practice of law based on a catalogue of errors, including "citation errors that made identification of the cases difficult." This reproach suggests an additional negative effect of citation errors: the court may become frustrated enough to ignore an incorrect citation altogether.

Some citation errors have brought financial consequences. Simple sloppiness was apparently the problem with one lawyer who was sanctioned in the amount of $32,000 for several missteps. *Pierotti v. Torian*. Among other things, he cited broadly to seven pages for one point and then wrote six pages of factual description that completely lacked citations. In another case, attorneys were sanctioned $750 under a state appellate rule for, among other things, typographical errors in citations to cases and to the record. *Hurlbert v. Gordon*. In imposing sanctions, the court remarked, "This type of 'laissez-faire' legal briefing falls far below the high standards of professionalism of the firm in question... [T]he briefing errors wasted the time of opposing counsel and hampered the work of the court." Another lawyer was required to pay the other side's costs and attorneys' fees partly because of citation errors. *Federated Mut. Ins. Co. v. Anderson*.

Citation errors can prompt critical comments, as when a court called briefs by both sides "of little value," partly because of their inaccurate citations. *Cook v. Hilltown Township.* The court said, "[T]he carelessness manifested by inaccurate citations is not in keeping with the tradition of the legal profession," adding that a traditional hallmark of "an outstanding legal brief [is] the accuracy of its citations." Elsewhere, a court called a brief of "minimal quality," noting that its "legal citations are inadequate or wrong." *McNeel v. Pub. Serv. Co.* Yet another court explained that "numerous" citation errors "in case names, subsequent history, volume and page numbers and jurisdictions...imposed an unwarranted burden on the court." *Weissman v. Fruchtman.* Another lawyer was no doubt embarrassed when a court found his brief "riddled with inaccurate and incomplete case citations" and lacking point cites. *Howard v. Oakland Tribune.* And the Illinois Court of Appeals recently reproached lawyers who cited the wrong reporters and left out page cites, explaining that correct citations "facilitate the administration of justice." *Ikari v. Mason Props.*

Several courts have chided attorneys for failure to adhere to the format prescribed in the *Bluebook. E.g., Billing v. City of Norfolk, Virginia; Cotter v. Helmer.* One court explained that correct citation format is necessary because it makes it easier for readers to follow citations. *Rodriguez v. Chen.*

CHAPTER 8

Follow Court Rules

Court rules exist to promote succinct, orderly briefs that judges can readily follow. For example, rules limiting the length of briefs "induce[ ] the advocate to write tight prose, which helps the client's cause." *Morgan v. South Bend Cmty. Sch. Corp.* Lawyers who flout court rules may find their briefs rejected or may encounter other negative consequences, as the following cases illustrate.

Follow Rules Regarding Page or Word Limits

Many trial and appellate courts now prescribe page or word limits on legal documents. Not surprisingly, counsel sometimes ignore or try to circumvent them. Some of the offending briefs are rejected at the filing window without leaving any published record. Other courts have stated on the record that they will not accept briefs that exceed the page limit. *Frazier v. Columbus Bd. of Educ.*; *Staffilino Chevrolet, Inc. v. Ohio Motor Vehicle Dealers Bd.* When excessively long briefs make it past the filing stage, they often prompt brusque remarks from the bench.

Do Not Exceed the Limit

Some courts that accepted long briefs have refused to consider language that exceeded the limit, *Columbus-America Discovery Group v. Atlantic Mut. Ins. Co.*; *Conkling v. Turner*, and some have also imposed sanctions, *State v. Hudson.* With others, the reaction is a rebuke on the record. For example, in In re *Personal Restraint of Lord,* excessively long briefs and appendices led the court to remark that "winnowing out weaker arguments" is a feature of effective advocacy.

Do Not Attempt to Circumvent the Limit

Some lawyers attempt to circumvent page limitations, a gambit the courts do not appreciate. The Ninth Circuit sanctioned one lawyer $1,500 for submitting a brief with lines typed one-and-one-half spaces apart instead of the required two spaces and with footnotes whose typeface and spacing violated the court's rule. *Kano v. Nat'l Consumer Co-op. Bank.* The Seventh Circuit fined other lawyers after it denied their request to file a longer brief and caught them trying to disguise their brief's length with impermissibly small spacing, typeface, and margins. *Westinghouse Elec. Corp. v. NLRB.* When ordered to file a complying brief, the lawyers moved "gobs of text" into single-spaced footnotes, incurring a $1,000 fine. Another court similarly fined a lawyer for improper line spacing to evade the page limit. *Doyle v. Hasbro, Inc.* Other lawyers incurred sanctions for using "minuscule" type to circumvent a page limit, *MacIntyre v. Butler,* and for putting much of a rejected brief in an appendix, *State v. Walden.*

Elsewhere, lawyers filed a brief that was "pocked with fifty-eight footnotes," many of which were lengthy and covered major arguments. Although the lawyers won the case, the court denied their motion for costs on appeal because their tactic had "blatantly evaded this court's page limit on briefs." *Varda, Inc. v. Ins. Co. of N. Am.*

Some lawyers' attempts to evade page limits caused their arguments to go unheard. One court ordered the clerk to strike motions that apparently were crafted to evade the page limit; the offending lawyers had filed four separate motions on the same point. *Novartis Consumer Health Inc., v. Elan Transdermal Technologies, Inc.* The court also issued an order to show cause why the lawyers should not be sanctioned. Another lawyer compressed line spacing to evade the page limit in a memorandum opposing summary judgment and then squeezed extra argument into the required concise statement of factual disagreements. *S Indus., Inc., v. JL Audio, Inc.* The court said it would not consider any legal arguments in that document.

In another case, a brief was stricken, although with leave to file a new one, where counsel engaged in the "undergraduate gambit" of shrinking typeface and footnotes and restarting page numbering several times to evade the page limit. *TK-7 Corp. v. Estate of Barbouti.* The court said,

> While we appreciate the savings in time and labor made possible by such technological innovations as word processing, we regret the temptation they pose to the wordy to compress, rather than edit.... Defendants will have to find some way of abridging their arguments, other than toying with their computers, to meet these requirements.

Another lawyer's "shotgun approach" was to set out the issues in a sentence or two and then refer the state supreme court to the appellate briefs, a technique that the court called "novel but nonetheless unacceptable" when it rejected the arguments so raised. *Indep. Sch. Dist. No. 622 v. Keene Corp.*

In other instances, attempts to circumvent the page limits have provoked disapproving comments. One lawyer was formally admonished when, after receiving an extension to the page limit, he filled his brief with inappropriate footnotes in order to submit yet more verbiage. *Alicia Z. v. Jose Z.* Another court reproached a lawyer who, after using up the pages allotted for his legal memorandum, attempted to bootstrap additional points into a long affidavit that was more argument than testimony. *Great Atl. & Pac. Tea Co. v. Town of E. Hampton.* And a court found it "especially vexing" that, after it denied a lawyer's motion to submit a longer brief, he submitted a brief with one and one-third spacing instead of the required double spacing. *Southern N.H. Water Co. v. Town of Hudson.*

Another court lamented that "laser printers and other typesetters have spread through law firms, leaving lawyers and their staffs to make decisions formerly in the hands of professional printers. This creates an opportunity to play games with type." *EDC v. Navistar Int'l Transp. Corp.* The brief that prompted this comment was so excessive, "shoehorning into the paper more words than the rules allowed," that the court declared it "bloated and argumentative" and filled with unnecessary tangential arguments. Although it did not sanction the lawyer, the court urged him to "brush up on the rules," adding "game-playing wastes the time of this court, time increasingly scarce as our docket grows at a rate exceeding 10% per year." Other courts have reprimanded lawyers for attempting to evade page limits by cramming material into single-spaced footnotes, *Anderson v. Alpha Portland Ind., Inc.*, manipulating spacing and fonts, *Anand v. National Republic Bank of Chicago*, and using small print, *Thomas & Betts Corp. v. Panduit Corp.*

Where court rules impose word limits instead of page limits, lawyers may try to circumvent those as well. One lawyer attempted to get around California's word limit by submitting a "combined brief," which is allowed where a case includes a cross-appeal. *Mitchell v. Holly Sugar Corp.* However, only 60 of the 19,500 words in the "combined" brief addressed the cross-appeal. The court "strongly disapprove[d]" of this tactic.

Some counsel have creatively argued that they could not include necessary material in their papers because of page limits. This notion has not found favor with the courts, several of which have declined to consider arguments that lawyers said they omitted because of length limitations. *Trust Co. v. N.N.P., Inc.*; *FTC v. World Travel Vacation Brokers, Inc.*; *State v. Bolton.*

File Papers on Time

Timeliness is paramount in the practice of law. Consequences of submitting late documents can be harsh: filings can be refused and claims lost. In one capital case, an appeal was dismissed where a lawyer filed the notice of appeal three days late. *Coleman v. Thompson.* And a civil appeal was dismissed because some of the required copies of the brief were a few minutes late. *Olander v. French.* A lawyer had arrived at the Ohio Supreme Court at 4:57 p.m. to file the brief. However, he had only fourteen of the required eighteen copies with him, and the office closed at 5:00 p.m. A secretary arrived with the others a few minutes after 5:00, but the clerk refused to accept them. On a motion to "retain this appeal," lawyers who worked on the brief offered several excuses, including a wedding anniversary, a daughter to be taken to college, editing and re-editing until the last minute, and a copier malfunction. The Ohio Supreme Court, however, was not moved. It dismissed the appeal on the ground that the brief was not timely filed.

Another lawyer lost his case because he was late filing papers after receiving four extensions. *Young v. City of Palm Bay.* Affirming a summary judgment against his client, the Eleventh Circuit pointed out that the lawyer's tardiness was inconsiderate of the court, the other parties, their counsel, and the legal system. The court lectured the lawyer further:

> Counsel must take responsibility for the obligations to which he committed and get work done by the deadline.... Deadlines are not meant to be aspirational; counsel must not treat the goodwill of the court as a sign that, as long as counsel tried to act, he has carte blanche to perform when he desires.

Recently the Texas Court of Appeals held that it lacked jurisdiction to hear a case where the notice of appeal was filed one day late. *Pickens v. State.* In another jurisdiction, a defendant's lawyer was more than a month late in filing a response to a motion for attorney's fees. *Ramseur v. Barreto.* A showing of excusable neglect would have allowed a court to consider the response, but the lawyer's only excuse was that he had inadvertently overlooked a key date. Accepting such an excuse would make the standard meaningless, the court said, and awarded the fees. Another lawyer missed the deadline for filing a notice of appeal and filed a motion for permission to file a late notice. *Sidwell Constr. Co. v. Dist. 837 Aeorspace Workers Credit Union.* That notice was one day late, prompting the court to dismiss the appeal with the sardonic comment that the "motion to file an untimely appeal was itself untimely." In another case, where a taxpayer's petition was filed by Federal Express rather than by mail as a court rule required, the taxpayer's suit was dismissed as untimely. *Fountain Parkway, Ltd. v. Tarrant Appraisal Dist.* And where one trial judge refused to accept an amended complaint filed one day late, his decision was upheld on appeal. *Taylor v. Lenawee County Bd. of Road Comm'rs.*

A familiar result of tardy filing is loss of a claim because the limitations period has run. Such attorney negligence may give rise to malpractice claims (*e.g.*, *Kohler v. Woollen, Brown & Hawkins*) or disciplinary proceedings (*e.g.*, *Hansen v. State Bar*). Where one suit was dismissed for untimely filing, the lawyer's excuse was that his runner had made a mistake. *Merrill v. Cintas Corp.* The judge nevertheless dismissed tardy claim, observing that the late filing was "a product of a decision to wait until the last day to file" and adding that in our system such attorney errors are attributed to clients.

Sanctions may also be imposed for untimely filing, especially after repeated offenses. Where one plaintiff's lawyer repeatedly missed deadlines, a trial judge declined to dismiss the case but fined the lawyer $1,000 plus costs and discoursed at some length about his conduct, labeling it "unjustified" and "contumacious." *Philips v. United States.*

Sometimes judges will overlook or excuse tardiness, but counsel count on leniency at their peril. One judge who had been lenient with time limits changed his approach. *Conn. Gen. Life Ins. Co. v. Chicago Title and Trust Co.* When two different lawyers belatedly asked his permission to file briefs "instanter," Judge Posner acknowledged that he had not always applied time limits strictly, but said he feared such "laxity" had caused delays and wasted the court's time. He therefore denied the motions and entered orders to show cause why the appeals should not be dismissed.

Violating Multiple Rules

Some lawyers incur courts' wrath by violating multiple rules. For one lawyer's violations, the Third Circuit took the harsh measure of dismissing an appeal. *Kushner v. Winterthur Swiss Ins. Co.* The lawyer had omitted documents required under rules "carefully drafted to assist a court burdened with a heavy case load." The court acknowledged its past reluctance to impose sanctions for nonconforming briefs, but having finally lost patience, it concluded, "Henceforth,...failure or unwillingness to master our procedures will necessarily result in the imposition of appropriate sanctions." The court said that the case before it was "another unhappy commentary on the professionalism of a relatively small number of lawyers who appear before us," adding that "the great bulk" of its cases "are handled by competent counsel."

Multiple rule violations may also bring sanctions. One lawyer was threatened with sanctions in a case that reminded a magistrate judge of "a back-alley knife fight." *Vandeventer v. Wabash Nat'l Corp.* The plaintiff's lawyers had brought baseless claims, while the defendant's lawyers failed to comply with a notice requirement, attempted to evade page limits through creative typography, and in general engaged in "gross overlitigation." The magistrate judge recommended sanctions, which would be set aside if the lawyers attended a continuing legal education seminar on Rule 11 or federal practice. The magistrate also attempted to "inspire introspection" by threatening possible future suspension from practice before the court.

CHAPTER 9

Do Not Plagiarize

Plagiarism by lawyers has not been discussed much in reported cases, but it recently led to a disciplinary action. *Iowa Supreme Court Bd. of Prof'l Ethics and Conduct v. Lane.* Attorney William Lane copied eighteen pages from a book into a brief he submitted to the court. He then made matters worse by asking the court to award him $16,000 in fees for preparing the brief. A magistrate suspected the brief was copied, and after Lane attempted to conceal his source, the magistrate found that Lane had taken "the legal portion of his brief verbatim" from the book. When the bar ethics board brought disciplinary proceedings against him, the state supreme court called his copying "plagiarism" and "unethical," explaining that "[w]e will not excuse the seriousness of passing off another's work as one's own." It added that Lane had intended to deceive and had "jeopardized the integrity of the Bar and the public's trust in the legal profession." The court suspended him from practice for six months and ordered him to pay the costs of the disciplinary action.

The *Lane* case does not completely clarify what constitutes unacceptable copying in law practice. Of course, any uncredited use of language from another source is plagiarism in the law school setting, where learning, evaluating student work, and protecting the intellectual record are the focus, as legal writing expert Terri LeClercq recently explained.[1] But the considerations are different in practice. In drafting complaints, agreements, and instruments, lawyers commonly check form books, which are meant to be consulted and par-

---

1. Terri LeClercq, *Failure to Teach: Due Process and Law School Plagiarism*, 49 J. LEGAL EDUC. 236, 250 (1999).

tially copied. Courts seem to accept this practice. For example, a state supreme court justice tacitly approved lawyers' use of boilerplate from "widely used model form books." *Moore v. Regents of the Univ. of Cal.* Some courts have even suggested that lawyers ought to consult forms: one court found a lawyer's claim of 2.8 hours for preparing a motion notice "exaggerated" because the notice "could easily have been copied from a form book," *Decibus v. Woodbridge Township Police Dept.*, while another court sent counsel a sample form from a book, *Politico v. Promus Hotels, Inc.*

Still, it is recognized good practice for an attorney who uses a form not to copy it uncritically but to exercise professional judgment to fit it to the particular need. One attorney who copied her complaint from a form book did not tailor it to her case and therefore failed to allege a requirement for her claim. *Clement v. Pub. Serv. Elec. & Gas Co.* The court dismissed the complaint and sternly pronounced that "[l]awyers are not automatons. They are trained professionals who are expected to exercise independent judgment." It also declared her performance below the standard of competence, publicly admonished her, and referred the case to disciplinary authorities.

In addition to using form books, lawyers sometimes prepare instruments by taking language from other lawyers' documents without attribution. At least one court approved of this practice: "Legal instruments are widely plagiarized, of course. We see no impropriety in one lawyer's adopting another's work, thus becoming the 'drafter' in the sense that he accepts responsibility for it." *Fed. Intermediate Credit Bank of Louisville v. Ky. Bar Ass'n.*

Briefs are different, though. They are supposed to represent a lawyer's analysis of a particular case, and courts have strongly disapproved the use of borrowed language in them. One lawyer was ordered to show cause why he should not be sanctioned for a brief that repeated large sections of a brief in another case almost verbatim. *USA Clio Biz, Inc., v. N.Y. State Dep't of Labor.* The court found the brief incomprehensible and factually inaccurate, which occurred because the lawyer copied much of the brief without any additional research or analysis relating to the pending case. The court found this conduct unacceptable. Another lawyer incurred a court's condemnation for plagiarism "wholly intolerable in the practice of law" when he copied large parts of opposing counsel's memorandum without adding any of his own research. *DeWilde v. Guy Gannett Publ'g Co.* The court disregarded the pleading and ordered the offending lawyer to pay the other side's attorneys' fees "for the services unwittingly rendered."

Significant factors in each of these cases were the large quantity of material copied and the lawyer's failure to do his own research on the subject. This points to a key difference between acceptable use of forms and Lane's conduct: a brief is supposed to present a lawyer's analysis, but Lane simply pasted large blocks of text into his brief without exercising professional judgment. This produced a brief that did little to address the issues in the specific case before the court.

Another significant difference between Lane's conduct and acceptable borrowing is the type of source used. While copying from form books is expected, treatises are not meant to be copied without attribution, and their uncredited use raises copyright issues. At least two courts have said that lifting material from treatises was plagiarism. *Kingvision Pay Per View, Ltd. v. Wilson; Frith v. State.* Another court found "intolerable" a lawyer's use of large blocks of text from a reported opinion without attribution. *Pagan Velez v. Laboy Alvarado.* In Lane's case, of course, there were two further exacerbating factors: Lane compounded his wrongdoing by requesting substantial fees for writing the document he copied, and he failed to be candid with the court when confronted about his conduct.

The *Lane* case puts lawyers on notice that copying unattributed material into papers filed with the court may result in disciplinary action.

CHAPTER 10

BE CIVIL

A century ago, Dean Roscoe Pound said, "The effect of our exaggerated contentious procedure is not only to irritate parties, witnesses, and jurors in particular cases, but to give the whole community a false notion of the purpose and end of law."[1] Today, when criticism of the legal profession abounds and "Rambo" litigation tactics have become too common (*see St. Paul Reinsurance Co. v. Commercial Fin. Co.*), Pound's words apply with special force. They emphasize that civility in lawyers' writing promotes high professional standards and benefits society by fostering the orderly resolution of disputes.

Several courts recently illustrated this principle when they met lawyers' ad hominem attacks with bar discipline. One lawyer, Gershater, was suspended indefinitely partly because she wrote a letter to her lawyer that was "vicious, offensive, and extremely unprofessional." In re *Gershater*. The court said the letter reflected poorly on Gershater's fitness to practice law, explaining that a lawyer should be able to "intelligently communicate his or her position without the use of profane, offensive, or derogatory language." Similarly, a lawyer whose brief suggested that judges had unethical motivations was publicly reprimanded for recklessly impugning the judges' integrity. In re *Wilkins*. And after a lawyer wrote, among other things, that a court referee had subjected him to a "high tech lynching" and was "intoxicated from his own whine," he received a formal admonition about his lack of civility. In re *Coe*.

---

1. Roscoe Pound, *The Causes of Popular Dissatisfaction with the Administration of Justice, in Proceedings in Commemoration of the Address Delivered Aug. 26, 1906 Before a Convention of the American Bar Association*, 35 F.R.D. 273, 282 (1964).

A court found it particularly offensive when a lawyer asserted in a motion that opposing counsel was the granddaughter of a controversial former dictator. *United States v. Kouri-Perez.* This statement revealed her adoption by another family, which by statute was supposed to remain confidential, and it also included a misrepresentation of fact. The news media immediately reported the story, which the offending lawyer may have leaked to the press. The court found his lack of civility unacceptable and assessed a fine of $4,000 against him, saying his conduct was "worthy of sanction [partly] because it unnecessarily intruded into the private life of a colleague and an officer of the court."

Another court upheld sanctions against a lawyer whose brief contained "classic ad hominem arguments," including a statement that he graduated from a law school that ranked higher than the school the opposing lawyer attended. *Greenfield v. First City Bancorporation of Tex., Inc.* And a case was remanded for sanctions after a lawyer discourteously described opposing counsel as firing "with a blunderbuss as much buckshot as possible." *Thomas v. Thomas.*

Ad hominem attacks drew a reproach and the threat of sanctions when an attorney's motion papers called the plaintiff a liar and said her counsel was "incapable of handling this litigation." *Cannon v. Cherry Hill Toyota.* The magistrate judge found that this constituted "impermissible recriminations," and stressed that lawyers "'are not free, like loose cannons, to fire at will upon any target of opportunity which appears on the legal landscape.'" *Id.*, quoting *Thomason v. Norman E. Lehrer, P.C.* The court pointed out that the excess verbiage used in such attacks serves neither the court, the client, nor the profession, and ordered the lawyer to explain in writing why he should not be sanctioned. Another lawyer's personal attacks, in which he called opposing counsel "'Nazis' and [']redneck peckerwood[s]'," combined with other offenses to merit a formal reprimand and an order to write an apology. *Lockheed Martin Energy Sys., Inc., v. Slavin.*

Another lawyer's papers stated that opposing counsel's motion rose "to the utmost level of absurdity" and was an "unbelievable demonstration of... 'chutzpah.'" *Griffith v. Hess Oil V.I. Corp.* The court found this language "not only unenlightening [but also] unnecessary and undignified" and exhorted attorneys to "conduct themselves professionally."

Obstructionist tactics also fall short of professional civility. Where a lawyer responded to discovery requests with objections that were "boilerplate, obstructionist, frivolous, overbroad" and contrary to the law, the judge remarked that such "'Rambo' style obstructionist discovery tactics… have a virus like potential to corrupt the fairness of our civil justice system." *St. Paul Reinsurance Co., Ltd. v. Commercial Fin. Corp.* The judge imposed an unusual sanction: he required the lawyer to write an article explaining why obstructionist discovery tactics are improper and submit it to law journals for publication.

In another case, a court reproached a lawyer for bringing a motion instead of making a courteous telephone call. The plaintiff's attorney had mistakenly refiled his first complaint as an amended complaint, and the defendant's attorney moved to dismiss it because the two complaints were identical. *Phila. Gear Corp. v. Swath Int'l, Ltd.* The court said the plaintiff's counsel should not have filed papers without reading them, but it also rebuked the defendant's counsel for not using the simple expedient of a telephone call to ascertain whether the duplicate complaint was filed in error. Emphasizing that "the law is a profession in which civility must be an essential element," the court added that "civility is the trademark of a winner." Lawyers would do well to live by those words.

Guidelines and Exercises

State the Law Accurately (Chapter 1)

Guidelines

Stating the law accurately requires attention to detail. A lawyer must do careful and thorough research and analyze the results to arrive at a correct understanding of what the authorities say. Then the lawyer must carefully choose wording to convey the content of the law accurately.

1. Research and analyze the law thoroughly. A careful research plan will help you research and analyze the law effectively. While a good plan will be tailored to the requirements of your specific issue, the example below suggests the kinds of steps you might consider incorporating in your plan. What amount of time you should devote to each step will depend on the complexity of the issue and amount of time you have to complete the document.

As you follow this plan, realize that research and writing are not a linear experience. After they begin to write, accomplished legal writers revisit steps in the research process to update material or to fill gaps in research.

Sample Research and Analysis Plan
Adapt this plan to fit your specific needs.

Step	Activity
1.	Identify and review secondary sources on your topic in both print and computer media. Goal: to obtain an overview of the topic.

2. Copy relevant statutes and cases that were identified in the secondary sources.
3. If a statute applies, check the annotated statute in hard copy or on line. Identify & copy relevant cases.
4. Read and annotate the copied cases.
5. Update the copied statutes and cases through Shepard's or Keycite. Note any important subsequent history; identify and print relevant cases.
6. Conduct a focused computer search for cases; print cases and note relevant key numbers.
7. Using the key numbers, check the print or on-line digest; identify and print relevant cases.
8. Read and annotate cases identified in steps 5–7.
9. Prepare a draft outline of the topic and check for weak spots in your research.
10. Check all accumulated material for relevant cases and secondary sources not already read; read and annotate any newly identified sources with an eye toward addressing weak spots.
11. Update all relevant cases.
12. Prepare an outline of the topic and prepare to write.
13. Repeat any of the above steps if necessary to complete your research.

How do you know you're finished researching? The following guidelines will help you determine whether you've done sufficient research.

- Have you followed all the steps in your research plan?
- Have you updated major cases?
- Have you checked the most recent cases on your topic to see what authorities they cite?
- Do you keep running across authorities that you've already discovered?

2. Be exact in reporting what the court said. Once you have a thorough analysis of the law, you must convey it to the reader. Below is some language lawyers use to describe courts' actions. Use language that conveys your precise meaning when describing these or other concepts.

Courts make *findings* of fact.

They issue *holdings* about the law. For example, a trial court may *grant* or *deny* a motion and *sustain* or *overrule* an objection. An appellate court may *overrule, affirm, reverse,* or *uphold* a decision of an inferior court.

Words like *conclude, decide,* and *determine* may describe courts' findings or holdings.

Some statements by courts are neither findings nor holdings. Courts may, for example, *agree, comment, condemn, disagree, emphasize, observe, point out, reason, say, state,* or *stress.*

Words like *argued* and *felt* are seldom appropriate to describe a court's statements. Lawyers argue and talk-show guests feel, but courts decide cases.

Some references on legal research

Robert C. Berring & Elizabeth A. Edinger, *Finding the Law* (11th ed. 1999)

Roy M. Mersky & Donald J. Dunn, *Fundamentals of Legal Research* (8th ed. 2002)

Exercises

Exercise 1-A.

Fill in each blank with a form of one of the italicized words on pages 58–59 that accurately conveys the concept. Refer to judges' or courts' actions in the past tense (for example, "the court *held*" or "*stressed*").

> After hearing the children's testimony, the trial judge _____ that they had been routinely abused. She also _____ that their mother had used illegal drugs daily for the previous five years. She therefore _____ that the mother's parental rights were terminated. The appellate court _____ that the mother was likely to continue her behavior. The court further _____ that the trial court's holding was consistent with applicable precedent cases, and it therefore _____ to _____ the trial judge's decision.

Exercise 1-B

A court found the following language in a lawyer's brief "dead wrong."
Read *Hernandez* and the two cases the lawyer cited in the passage
below and rewrite the passage so that it accurately reflects the cases'
content. Reflect the law accurately even if you conclude that it does
not support the lawyer's position.

> "The federal courts...have...consistently accorded preclu-
> sive effect to issues decided by state courts." *Allen v. McCurry,*
> 449 U.S. 90, 95 (1980). Furthermore, "when a state agency
> 'acting in a judicial capacity...resolves disputed issues of fact
> properly before it which the parties have had an adequate op-
> portunity to litigate,' federal courts must give the agency's
> fact finding the same preclusive effect to which it would be
> entitled in the State's courts." *University of Tenn. v. Elliott,* 478
> U.S. 788, 799 (1986).

Hernandez v. N.Y. Law Dept. Corp. Counsel, No. 94 Civ. 9042 (AJP)
(SS), 1997 WL 270047, at *14 and n.11 (S.D.N.Y. Jan. 23, 1997).

State the Facts Accurately (Chapter 2)

Guidelines

Stating facts accurately requires careful attention to exact word
choice. For example, if a case opinion says the defendant "glanced
at" a document, do not write that the defendant "read" it. The two
words have different meanings that may have legal significance in
certain contexts. Consult a good legal dictionary for definitions of
legal terms.

Suggested legal dictionaries:

Bryan A. Garner, *A Dictionary of Modern Legal Usage* (Oxford
Univ. Press 2d ed. 1995)
Black's Law Dictionary (Bryan A. Garner ed., West 7th ed. 1999)

Provide Cogent Analysis (Chapter 3)

Guidelines

One cause of faulty legal analysis is the use of fallacious reasoning. Familiarize yourself with the following fallacies and practice avoiding them.

Fallacies

Writers at times slip into *fallacies*—that is, illogical reasoning that invites a wrong inference or is misleading. Some types of fallacies occur frequently enough to have acquired common names, some of which are listed below. You should avoid them in your writing.

Arguing ad hominem is attacking an opponent personally instead of disproving his or her point. Example: "Because the senator has been accused of campaign irregularities, his social security proposal should be defeated."

Begging the question is basing a conclusion on a principle that needs to be proven as much as the conclusion itself. Example: "Democracy must be the best form of government because the majority is always right." (Note: "Begs the question" does *not* mean "invites the obvious question.")

Circular reasoning is basing two conclusions on each other. Example: "We know the judge is wise because he correctly interpreted the law. We know he correctly interpreted the law because he is wise." (This is a form of begging the question).

The **either-or fallacy** implies that only two alternatives exist when actually there are more than two. Example: "You must use professional slides in the courtroom or lose your case."

Equivocation means using a word in two senses in close proximity. Example: "The court will not sanction such behavior from a member of the bar. Therefore, the court will sanction counsel in the amount of $500."

False analogy means identifying a similarity between two things and then concluding that the two are equal in other, irrelevant respects. Example: "Because each of these student papers is four pages long, they should receive the same grade."

Mixing metaphors means putting two metaphors in such close proximity that they conflict. Example: "Counsel has buried his head in the sand and ridden roughshod over the statutory scheme."

Non sequitur is a Latin phrase meaning "it does not follow." It refers to a conclusion that does not follow from what was previously stated. Example: "Smith was negligent when he hit Henderson with his car. Therefore, Henderson should sue Smith for breach of contract."

Post hoc ergo propter hoc means "after which, therefore because which." It is the fallacy of confusing sequence with consequence. Example: "In the last hundred years, all Presidents elected in years ending with zero have either died or been shot while in office, or both. Therefore, being elected President in a year ending in zero causes one to die or to be shot in office."

Some references on legal analysis

Thomas C. Marks, Jr., *Understanding the Process of Judicial Policy Making through Case Analysis*, 29 Stetson L. Rev. 1155 (2000)

Helene Shapo & Marshall Shapo, *Law School Without Fear: Strategies for Success* 59–86 (2d ed. 2002)

Exercise 3

Identify the fallacy in each item below.

Name of Fallacy

_____ 1. A reasonable person is a person who reasons well.

_____ 2. The plaintiff was not wearing a seat belt when she was injured in the accident. Her own conduct, then, was the cause of her injuries.

_____ 3. Punitive damages awards have become excessively large. Therefore, the plaintiff has not proven sufficient facts to recover punitive damages here.

_____ 4. Judge Worth belongs to the Green Party. Therefore, his decisions should carry no weight.

_____ 5. The buyer showed a complete lack of consideration for the seller when she failed to provide consideration for their contract.

_____ 6. If you come on board with our firm, we'll expect you to put your nose to the grindstone and your shoulder to the wheel.

_____ 7. The defendant's conduct was so despicable that reasonable persons would view it as egregious. Because the conduct was egregious, it fulfills the despicable conduct requirement of the punitive damages statute.

_____ 8. Abortion is murder. Therefore, because murder is illegal, abortion should also be illegal.

Write Clearly, Avoiding Wordiness and Legalese (Chapters 4–5)

Guidelines

The following guidelines will help you rid your writing of wordiness and legalese.

1. Eliminate unnecessary words by using these three methods:

   A. Strike out excess words.

      Enclosed ~~herein~~ is Exhibit A.

      He will sign each ~~and every~~ document.

   B. Rewrite a phrase:

      Not this: For the reason that he had no evidence on his side, he decided to plead guilty.

      Better: Because he had no evidence on his side, he decided to plead guilty.

   C. Restructure the entire sentence:

      Not this: It would seem that an incorrect analysis of the issue has been advanced.

      Better: The court's analysis was incorrect.

2. Use ordinary English words to replace outdated lawyers' language (often called "legalese").

   Not this: The party of the first part affixed his signature to the aforementioned contract.

   Better: The buyer signed the contract.

3. Be direct. To make writing more direct, use simpler language, more concrete nouns, and the active voice.

   Not this: Consideration of court determinations compels the conclusion that outrageousness is evaluated on the basis of the totality of the factual circumstances.

   Better: In deciding whether conduct is outrageous, courts consider the totality of the circumstances.

4. Avoid using the passive voice unless you have a good reason to use it. (In the passive voice, the subject is the receiver of the

action and the verb contains some form of the verb *be*. For example: The motion was argued by Wilson.)

Not this: The validity of the signature was testified to by Mr. Brown.

Better: Mr. Brown testified that the signature was valid.

5. Avoid clumsy nouns constructed from verbs. Try substituting the verb form to make a stronger statement.

   Not this: What conclusion have you drawn about the case?

   Better: What have you concluded about the case?

6. Although long sentences can be effective, they are often clumsy and hard to follow. Consider breaking them up into smaller units.

   Not this: In *Haverly*, the plaintiffs alleged that the defendant manufacturer's failure to test a particular type of seat belt buckle after a "position paper" warned of possible design flaws in the buckle and after outside testing revealed possible defects in the buckle constituted despicable conduct justifying punitive damages.

   Better: In *Haverly*, both a position paper and outside testing warned the manufacturer that a seat belt buckle might be defective. Yet the manufacturer failed to test it. The court held that this constituted despicable conduct, justifying punitive damages.

Some references on eliminating wordiness and legalese

Bryan A. Garner, *The Elements of Legal Style* (2d ed. 2002)
Terri LeClercq, *Legal Writing Style* (3d ed. 2004)
William Strunk, Jr. & E.B. White, *The Elements of Style* (4th ed. 2000)
Richard Wydick, *Plain English for Lawyers* (4th ed. 1998).

Exercises

Judges criticized the writing in the following examples. Rewrite them to respond to the judges' objections.

Exercise 4A

Rewrite this language from a statute, which a court called a "virtually impenetrable thicket of legalese"

> [a] State plan for medical assistance must—…include…reasonable standards…for determining eligibility for and the extent of medical assistance under the plan which (A) are consistent with the objectives of this title, (B) provide for taking into account only such income and resources as are, as determined in accordance with standards prescribed by the Secretary, available to the applicant or recipient and (in the case of any applicant or recipient who would, except for income and resources, be eligible for aid or assistance in the form of money payments under any plan of the State approved under title I, X, XIV, or XVI or part A of title IV, or to have paid with respect to him supplemental security income benefits under title XVI) as would not be disregarded (or set aside for future needs) in determining his eligibility for such aid, assistance or benefits, (C) provide for reasonable evaluation of any such income or resources, and (D) do not take into account the financial responsibility of any individual for any applicant or recipient of assistance under the plan unless such applicant or recipient is such individual's spouse or such individual's child who is under 21 or…is blind or permanently and totally disabled, or is blind or disabled…; and provide for flexibility in the application of such standards with respect to income by taking into account, except to the extent prescribed by the Secretary, the costs…incurred for medical care or for any other type of remedial care recognized under State law.

Lamore v. Ives

Exercise 4B

A court said this example from a complaint contained "repetitive, speculative, vague and general allegations." Rewrite it to eliminate those problems.

COUNT IV: COMMON LAW INDEMNITY AGAINST THE RMV

43. The RMV undertook a negligent course of conduct in connection with its lease and occupation of the Ruggles Center from Ruggles LLC, which negligence included, but is not limited to, the negligent supervision of its employees and agents; the negligent hiring and/or supervision of various entities who performed work at the Ruggles Center; and negligent conduct with respect to the construction, occupation, coordination and modification of the Ruggles Center.

44. The aforementioned negligent conduct committed by the RMV adversely affected the HVAC systems and/or the fireproofing and/or the overall health and/or environmental condition of the Ruggles Center and caused the damages alleged by Ruggles LLC and Beacon.

COUNT XXVIII: INDEMNIFICATION AGAINST COSENTINI

163. At all times relevant hereto, Cosentini was involved in the designing and/or manufacture and/or installing and/or supplying and/or planning and/or modifying and/or remediation of the HVAC and/or electrical systems at the Ruggles Center.

164. Cosentini was negligent in connection with its involvement in designing and/or manufacture and/or installing and/or supplying and/or planning and/or modifying and/or remediation of the HVAC and/or electrical systems at the Ruggles Center.

Ruggles Center, LLC v. Beacon Constr. Co.

Exercise 4C

A judge called these objections to a discovery request "boilerplate" and a " 'Rambo' style obstructionist discovery tactic[ ]" and ordered the offending attorney to write an article for bar publications explaining why his response was inappropriate. Review the laws on discovery responses in your jurisdiction and apply them while editing these responses to make them more succinct.

DOCUMENT REQUEST NO 1: All documents identified, or relied on, in your answers to Counterclaim Plaintiff's First Set of Interrogatories Directed to Counterclaim Defendant.

OBJECTIONS TO DOCUMENT REQUEST NO. 1: St. Paul objects to this request on the ground that the request is oppressive, burdensome and harassing. St. Paul further objects to this request on the ground that it is vague, ambiguous and unintelligible. St. Paul further objects that the request is overbroad and without reasonable limitation in scope or time frame. St. Paul further objects that the request seeks information that is protected from disclosure by the attorney-client privilege, the attorney work product doctrine and/or the joint interest or joint defense privilege. St. Paul further objects to this request on the ground that the request seeks information and documents equally available to the propounding parties from their own records or from records which are equally available to the propounding parties. St. Paul further objects that this request fails to designate the documents to be produced with reasonable particularity

DOCUMENT REQUEST NO. 4: All contracts, agreements, or communications of any kind by and/or between you and Iowa Banker's Insurance and Services, Inc.

OBJECTIONS TO DOCUMENT REQUEST NO. 4: St. Paul objects to this request on the ground that the information and documents requested are neither relevant to the subject matter of this action nor reasonably calculated to lead to the discovery of admissible evidence. St. Paul further objects that the request is oppressive, burdensome and harassing. St. Paul further objects [to] this request on the ground that it is vague, ambiguous and unintelligible. St. Paul further objects that the request is overbroad and without reasonable limitation in scope of time frame. St. Paul further objects that this request fails to designate the documents to be produced with reasonable particularity.

DOCUMENT REQUEST NO. 5: All contracts or agreements between you and U.S. Risk Underwriters, Inc.

OBJECTIONS TO DOCUMENT REQUEST NO. 5: St. Paul objects to this request on the ground that the information and documents requested are neither relevant to the subject matter of this action nor reasonably calculated to lead to discovery of admissible evidence. St. Paul further objects that the request is oppressive, burdensome and harassing. St. Paul further objects that the request is overbroad and without reasonable limitation in scope or time frame. St. Paul further objects that this request fails to designate the documents to be produced with reasonable particularity.

St. Paul Reinsurance Co. v. Commercial Fin. Co., 198 F.R.D. 508 (N.D. Iowa 2000)

Exercise 4D

The following set of interrogatories breaks many guidelines for clarity and conciseness. It was written by a new lawyer for a supervising partner. The case involved a large sum of money that one corporation ("Widget Corporation") claimed another corporation ("Manufacturers, Ltd.") owed due to dealings with a third corporation ("Acme Corporation"). The names and identifying information have been changed, and only some of the interrogatories are included, but otherwise the interrogatories appear as they were written. Read them and answer the questions beginning at page 72. Then read the sample that follows and edit the remainder of the set as requested at page 74.

Example for Exercise 4D: Wordy, ineffective interrogatories

COURT OF COMMON PLEAS FOR THE STATE
OF FRANKLIN, COUNTY OF HANCOCK

WIDGET CORPORATION, LTD., et al.,	) CASE NO. 12345
	)
	)
Plaintiffs,	)
	) FIRST SET OF
	) INTERROGATORIES
	) PROPOUNDED TO
	) DEFENDANT
vs.	) ACME CORPORATION
	) OF PLEASANTVILLE,
	) U.S.A. BY PLAINTIFF
	) WIDGET CORPORA-
MANUFACTURERS, LTD.,	) TION, LTD.
etc., et al.,	)
Defendants.	)
	)

TO DEFENDANT ACME CORPORATION OF PLEASANTVILLE, U.S.A., AND TO ITS ATTORNEYS OF RECORD HEREIN:

The Plaintiff, WIDGET CORPORATION, LTD., requires that Defendant, ACME CORPORATION OF PLEASANTVILLE, U.S.A., provide fully responsive answers under oath to the following Interrogatories within thirty (30) days of service hereof, in accordance with and pursuant to the provisions of Franklin Code § 288.

DEFINITIONS

The following definitions apply to each of the interrogatories hereinafter set forth and are deemed to be incorporated by reference therein:

A. "You" and "your," and each of them as the case may be, mean and refer to the defendant, ACME CORPORATION OF PLEAS-ANTVILLE, U.S.A.

B. "ACME CORPORATION" means and refers to ACME CORPORATION OF PLEASANTVILLE, U.S.A., a defendant in the above-entitled action.

C. "The Simons letter" shall mean and refer to the letter written January 15, 2002 by Malcolm P. Simons to Hancock County Judge Chandler W. Wise.

D. "The Wentworth letter" shall mean and refer to the letter written dated January 2, 2002 by Clark N. Wentworth to Ms. Dorothea Collins regarding Widget Corporation v. Manufacturers, Ltd.

E. "Person" and "persons," and each of them as the case may be, mean and refer to any natural person, firm, association, corporation, partnership, estate, and any other group or combination acting as a unit of more than one (1) natural person or any other form of legal entity.

F. "Document" means and includes reproduced and recorded types of written, typed, printed, reproduced and recorded matter, describing or pertaining, referring or relating, directly and indirectly, and in whole or in part, to the matter referred to in the interrogatory, and includes documents in your possession or custody, or under the control of you and/or your agents, servants, employees, representatives and all manner of persons associated with you. The above term includes, without limitation, each letter, note, item of correspondence, contract, agreement, file, record, recording, tape, photograph, drawing, memorandum, order, analysis, study, and any and all notations on the foregoing and/or copies thereof, as well as each summary or report by whomsoever prepared, regarding the act, event, or matter which is the subject of the Interrogatory.

G. "Communication" and "oral communication," and each of them, unless otherwise specified in any of the following Interrogatories, mean and refer to any non-written method or means of transmitting or receiving information or words, directly and indirectly, personally and by mechanical means, and includes the actual information and words transmitted and received.

H. "Identify" when used with reference to a person, requires you to state the following: (a) the person's name; (b) his present or last known home address and home telephone number; (c) his business affiliation as of the date of the transaction or event referred to; and, (d) his present business position or title and, if known to you, his present business address and telephone number.

I. "Describe in full detail," or "state all facts," when used in, as part of, or in connection with an Interrogatory, requires you to set out every aspect of every fact, act, omission, conduct, event, transaction, meeting or occasion concerning which you have knowledge or information, including, without limitation, the place and date thereof, the identity of each person present thereat, connected with or having knowledge thereof, the subject matter involved therein, and, if anything were communicated by any person, an identification and setting forth of each communication, if the same, in whole or in part, constituted or was contained or reported, summarized or referred to, in any document, then and in that event you are required to identify each such document.

INTERROGATORIES

1. In Paragraph 5 of your Complaint you allege that "It is evident that Manufacturers, Ltd. during 2000...repaid itself $576,000.50." State all facts upon which you base that allegation.

2. State whether you have retained any person, firm or corporation to review the general ledgers dated 1997 through 2003 and general journal entries made available by Manufacturers, Ltd. If so, identify such person, firm or corporation.

3. If any person, firm, or corporation referred to in the preceding response has provided you with a written report, identify the same.

4. Paragraph 2 of the Wentworth letter states that "You will recall that we had previously established that sums due Acme Corporation were properly accrued by Manufacturers, Ltd. at 6.5 percent of gross revenue but only a portion thereof was remitted during the years 1997, 1998, 1999, 2000, 2001, 2002, and 2003." With reference to the statement in question, state in full detail the following:

   a. By what means this was established;

   b. If this was established by a written report, identify the same;

   c. The meaning of the term "only a portion thereof was remitted" as you employed that term in the statement above;

   d. The identities of any and all persons who allegedly established this information; and

   e. The identities of any and all persons who communicated with Acme Corporation respecting this statement or the "establishment" of this information.

5. Paragraph 2 of the Wentworth letter states that "The most part of the accrued amount was reversed at the year-end, reducing the set-up expense and thereby increasing the net income of each subsidiary company." With reference to that statement, state in full detail the following:

   a. The meaning of the term "the most part" as you employed that term in the above statement;

   b. State all facts upon which you base that statement;

   c. The identities of any and all persons who made the statement in question; and

   d. The identities of any and all persons who communicated with National Union respecting the statement made above.

[This example ends here, although the actual document was longer.]

Questions:

1. How would you react if you were one of the following persons reading the above interrogatories:

    a. The assigning partner who asked a junior lawyer to write them,

    b. The lawyer for Acme Corporation, who is being asked to answer them, or

    c. The judge who is supervising this case?

2. Which is more likely to prompt an effective response: the set of interrogatories above, or a less wordy set?

Example: Editing clumsy, wordy interrogatories

The supervising partner was not pleased with the interrogatories on the previous pages and sent them back for editing.

Below is a suggested edited version of the "Definitions" section up to and including definition F ("document").

Rewritten Definitions

DEFINITIONS

The following definitions apply to these interrogatories.

Comments

This language eliminates legalese and unnecessary words.

[The definition of "You" and "your" is omitted.]

Defining "you" and "your" adds nothing because the interrogatories are already addressed to Acme Corporation.

1. "ACME CORPORATION" means ACME CORPORATION OF PLEASANTVILLE, U.S.A., a defendant in this action.

This sentence eliminates the redundant pair "mean and refer to."

2. "THE SIMONS LETTER" means the letter dated January 15, 2002 which is addressed to Judge Chandler W. Wise and bears the signature "Malcolm P. Simons."

The revised sentence describes the letter without assuming who wrote it, a fact not yet proven. It also eliminates the superfluous future tense "shall."

3 "THE WENTWORTH LET-TER" means the letter dated

January 2, 2002 which is addressed to Ms. Dorothea Collins
regarding Widget Corporation
v. Manufacturers, Ltd. and
bears the signature "Clark N.
Wentworth."

4. The terms "Person" and "Persons" include both natural persons and other legal entities such
   as corporations and partnerships.

This sentence defines the terms without the unnecessary language.

5. "Writing" is used as defined in
   Franklin Evidence Code § 153.

This definition refers to the state evidence code, an approach you can take if your jurisdiction has defined a term like "writing."

Directions for Exercise 4D

Rewrite the rest of the set of interrogatories, including the definitions after definition F, paying special attention to the guidelines above. There is not just one way to rewrite these interrogatories. Use your common sense to produce a more effective set of interrogatories. Do not be concerned about the substance of the case; this exercise focuses on writing, so work with the information that is given in the unedited interrogatories.

Of course, when you prepare interrogatories, you must follow any relevant rules in your jurisdiction; note, for example, that some jurisdictions do not allow subparts.

Avoid Grammar, Spelling, Punctuation, and Typographical Errors (Chapter 6)

A. Grammar

Guidelines

The following guidelines will help you avoid some common grammatical errors.

1. *Avoid misplaced modifiers.* Modifiers should be placed as close as possible to the word or phrase they modify.

   Not this: The defendant's lawyer only argued for a fine of $300.

   Better: The defendant's lawyer argued for a fine of only $300.

2. *Avoid dangling modifiers.* A modifier at the beginning of a sentence must modify the grammatical subject.

   Not this: After considering both motions, the case was dismissed.

   Better: After considering both motions, the judge dismissed the case.

3. *Use parallel construction where English grammar requires it.* Parallel elements should be expressed as the same parts of speech.

   Not this: The lawyer planned to make phone calls, finish a brief, and the library.

   Better: The lawyer planned to make phone calls, finish a brief, and go to the library.

4. *A pronoun must agree in number with a nearby antecedent.*

   Not this: The *Klein* case is distinguishable from Rose's case because their negligence lasted over a period of months.

   Better: The *Klein* case is distinguishable from Rose's case because the Kleins' negligence lasted over a period of months.

5. *Avoid run-on sentences and comma splices.* A compound sentence has two or more independent clauses, each of which has a subject and a verb and can stand alone as a sentence. The

parts of a compound sentence may be connected only two ways: by a coordinate conjunction or by a semi-colon. Coordinate conjunctions are *and, or, nor, but, for, so,* and *yet.* A comma alone is not an appropriate way to connect independent clauses.

Not this: The judge granted the motion to dismiss she then granted the plaintiff leave to amend. (This is a run-on sentence, that is, two independent clauses with no connector.)

Not this: The judge granted the motion to dismiss, however she then granted the plaintiff leave to amend. (This is a comma-splice, that is, two independent clauses without a proper connector. *However* is not a coordinate conjunction.)

Better: The judge granted the motion to dismiss, but she then granted the plaintiff leave to amend.

Or: The judge granted the motion to dismiss; she then granted the plaintiff leave to amend.

6. *Use the correct tense.*

- Express courts' statements and actions in the past tense:

Not this: The court concludes that the defendant is lying.
Better: The court concluded that the defendant was lying.

- Express current general principles in the present tense:

The court pointed out that perjury is an indictable offense.

- Use the past perfect tense (*had* plus a verb form) to indicate that an action happened before some identifiable past time.

Not this: The judge had denied the motion to exclude evidence. (This is incorrect if there is no nearby reference to a past time).

Better: The judge had denied the motion to exclude evidence, but he later changed his mind.

Some references on English grammar

Anne Enquist & Lauren Currie Oates, *Just Writing* (2001)

Diana Hacker, *A Writer's Reference* (4th ed. 1999)

Winifred Bryan Horner et al., *Hodges' Harbrace Handbook* (13th ed. 1998)

Ann Raimes, *Keys for Writers: A Brief Handbook* (3d ed. 2002)

Exercise 6A

Identify the grammatical errors in the sentences below and correct them.

1. The court handed down their opinion on Monday.
2. After researching the question, it appears that the plaintiff has a viable claim.
3. In 1970, the court holds that Smith proved racial discrimination.
4. The lawyer developed a careful analysis of the law on punitive damages, he then argued that only compensatory damages were appropriate in the pending case.
5. She researched the problem by reading secondary sources, copying cases, and a computer search.
6. Focusing on the issue of intent, the actions of the defendant seem to demonstrate only negligence.
7. When the statute was amended, they added a limitation on damages for pain and suffering.
8. Good writing should be easy to read, interesting, and should flow from one subject to another.
9. The witness calmly told his story, however he omitted key facts.
10. In explaining its holding, the court states that it must deny the motion for procedural reasons.

B. Spelling and Proofreading
Guidelines

According to recent research, the greatest difference between law students who wrote good briefs and those who wrote weak ones was that the stronger students spent significantly more time revising and proofreading.[1] So it is important to allow enough time for this process.

When you are proofreading, it is easy to overlook spelling and typographical errors in your own writing. To counteract this tendency, try the following techniques:

---

1. Anne M. Enquist, *Unlocking the Secrets of Why Some Legal Writing Students are Highly Successful, Moderately Successful, or Only Marginally Successful Writers,* Presentation at the 2004 Conference of the Legal Writing Institute.

1. While you are writing a document, use a symbol (such as a double asterisk) to mark items you want to check later. When the document is almost finished, perform a computer search for your symbol to be certain you've caught all the things you wanted to check.
2. Run computer grammar-check and spell-check programs. Do be aware, though, that you must exercise judgment about the suggestions these programs offer. The computer will not recognize some rather complex but appropriate grammatical constructions. For example, one computer program would not accept the word *Smiths'*. This usage is appropriate for a plural possessive, but the computer instead suggested using either *Smith's* or *Smith*, both of which were incorrect in the particular context. Computers may also challenge accurate spellings, especially of legal terms. You should reject many of the suggestions the computer makes, but running grammar- and spell-check programs is worthwhile because they may help you catch a few errors that escaped your eye.
3. When the document is almost finished, put it aside for at least twenty-four hours to gain some perspective. Then reread it, looking for errors you may have missed.
4. Imagine that you are another person reading your document. Ask yourself, "How would a judge [or senior partner, or professor] view this document?" Then look at it again from that perspective.
5. To provide fresh perspective for catching errors, read the document backwards from the end.
6. Scan the document visually or by computer for your own common errors, such as particular spelling mistakes.
7. Read the document aloud, perhaps to another person.
8. Have your computer read the document aloud through a program such as Microsoft Word's Narrator or ReadPlease.com. Your ear may catch errors that your eye missed.
9. "Eyeball" your document before declaring it finished. That is, glance over it for problems that you may not have noticed on a closer reading. Pay special attention to the first and last pages

and the overall organization. Check subheadings to see whether they are parallel and follow a logical sequence. They should fit together coherently, giving an overview of your analysis.

When you proofread, have good reference books at hand, including a general dictionary, a law dictionary, and a reference book on grammar and punctuation. Use them freely.

Exercise 6B

Judges pointed out spelling and proofreading errors in the following passages through the use of *sic.* Correct the errors.

> Kenneth Trapp and Karen Trapp (hereinafter appellants), minors under 14 years of age, by Kenneth Trapp and Rose Trapp, their parents, allege in their first amended complaint for negligent infliction of emotional distress that they are the first cousins of Ian Glenn McSweaney, with whom they "had a very close emotional attattchment [sic]." It is further alleged that appellants and McSweaney "played together often and had a relationship analagous [sic] to a relationship between siblings. Plaintffs [sic] loved [McSweaney] as they would their own brother." Appellants brought this action after sustaining "great emotional distrubance [sic] and shock and injury to their nervous system [sic], resulting in gastrointestinal disorders, head aches [sic], shock, anxiety, and loss of sleep."
> *Trapp v. Schuyler Constr.*

> As for there being typos, yes there have been typos, but these errors have not detracted from the arguments or results, and the rule in this case was a victory for Mr. Devore. Further, had the Defendants not tired [sic] to paper Plaintiff's counsel to death, some type [sic] would not have occurred. Furthermore, there have been omissions by the Defendants, thus they should not case [sic] stones.
> *Devore v. City of Phila.*

C. Punctuation

Master the guidelines below and you will be able to solve most of the comma issues that arise in legal writing.

The comma—guidelines

1. Use commas to separate items in a series of more than two.

   Example: The lawyer introduced live testimony, videotaped testimony, and documentary evidence.

2. Use a comma before a coordinate conjunction to link main clauses.

   Example: The defendant acted in conscious disregard of the plaintiff's rights, but his conduct was not despicable.

3. Use a comma after an introductory phrase or clause unless it is very short.

   Examples:

   To support an award of punitive damages in a nonintentional tort case, a defendant's conduct must be despicable.

   In Maine, a different rule applies.

   Or, In Maine a different rule applies.

4. Use commas to set off nonrestrictive parenthetical elements. A restrictive element is *limiting*; a nonrestrictive element is *descriptive.*

   Examples:

   Lawyers who steal from clients should be disbarred. (*Who steal from clients* is not set off by commas because it is a restrictive modifier—it limits the subject. The sentence therefore applies only to certain lawyers, those who steal from clients.)

   Lawyers, who belong to an honorable profession, should observe strict ethical guidelines. (*Who belong to an honorable profession* is set off by commas because it is a nonrestrictive modifier—it is merely descriptive. The sentence therefore applies to all lawyers).

   Each of the above examples would have a different meaning if it were punctuated differently.

5. Use a comma after a conversational tag that introduces a quotation.

    Example: The judge said, "Case dismissed."

6. Always have a reason for adding a comma. If you cannot identify a rule requiring one, chances are the comma does not belong there.

    • Do not add a comma just because you use a conjunction.

      Not this: The court found that intent was lacking, and dismissed the case.

      Not this: The judge ordered the lawyer to arrive on time, but, he was late. (The second comma is incorrect.)

    • Do not add a single comma between the subject and the verb.

      Not this: The judge who had recently been appointed to the bench, dismissed the case.

    • Do not add a comma just because the sentence seems out of control. If it's out of control, rewrite it.

      Not this: The governing statute and the cases discussed below indicate that a plaintiff attempting to prove malice in a case where intentional conduct is not alleged, must satisfy two essential elements.

Exercise 6C—The Comma

In the following passage, circle every incorrect comma and add new commas where they are needed. Explain why you made each decision.

Earl Warren held important offices on both the state, and national levels. As the governor of California for three successive terms Warren signed important laws, and oversaw improvements in the state's infrastructure. He was a successful governor, however, he aspired to higher positions. He first tried for national office as the Republican vice-presidential candidate in the 1948 election but, the Democrat Truman, won the election by a close margin. However that was not the end of his national prominence. In 1953 the next president Eisenhower appointed Warren to the Supreme Court. As Chief Justice, Warren presided over many landmark cases including *Brown v. Board of Education.* Explaining Warren's ability to inspire others biographer Ed Cray wrote "His leadership stemmed from personal vision ...." In addition to sitting on the court Warren chaired the commission that investigated the death of President Kennedy. That commission issued a report, that has inspired numerous articles books and films.

The apostrophe—guidelines

1. Apostrophes do *not* belong in
   * ordinary plural nouns.

     Not this: The juror's voted to acquit the defendant.
     Correct: The jurors voted to acquit the defendant.

   * plural names (unless they are possessive)

     Not this: The Kempers' were a loving family.
     Correct: The Kempers were a loving family.

   * Possessive personal pronouns

     Not this: This book is her's. It's cover is blue.
     Correct: This book is hers. Its cover is blue.

2. Apostrophes *do* belong in possessive nouns. (The possessive case denotes possession or connection: Jessica's desk; the chair's leg.)
   * Singular nouns (no *s* ending): add 's

     Mike's money will cover the filing fee.
     The judge's courtroom is upstairs.
     The book's cover was soiled.

   * Singular nouns ending in and *s* or *z* sound: Add 's unless the result would be hard to pronounce, in which case add ' only:

     James's intent
     Demosthenes' speech

- Plural nouns ending in s: add '

  Take this to the lawyers' lounge.

  The court ruled in favor of states' rights.

  The Andersons' car was repossessed.

  But: the women's room.

Some references on punctuation

Anne Enquist & Lauren Currie Oates, *Just Writing* (2001)
Diana Hacker, *A Writer's Reference* (4th ed. 1999)
Winifred Bryan Horner et al., *Hodges' Harbrace Handbook* (13th ed. 1998)
Terri Le Clercq, *Legal Writing Style* (3d ed. 2004)
Ann Raimes, *Keys for Writers: A Brief Handbook* (3d ed. 2002)

Exercise 6D—The Apostrophe

Add any necessary apostrophes to the paragraph below and explain your reasoning:

> The Kellers marriage had reached a breaking point when Al Keller contacted attorney Jim Smith about a dissolution. Smith met with Al the next week to go over the facts of the Kellers case. Because Smiths knowledge of recent tax cases was weak, he contacted attorney Meg Bryants office about the Kellers tax situation. Smith and Bryant concluded that the Kellers would have to sell Als Porsche after having its tires replaced. Smith also arranged to see the Kellers house; he recommended that the Kellers have its roof fixed and sell it. Finally, though, it was the Kellers antique lamps that caused the couples greatest disagreement. Al Kellers mood worsened, and Smith gave him several psychiatrists names.

Cite Correctly (Chapter 7)

Citing Cases—A Short Guide Through the Maze

In our system of precedent-based law, a lawyer's opinion has little or no weight. Accurate citations to legal sources provide the grounding in precedent that is necessary to convince a court. Lawyers follow prescribed citation rules as a "code" that lets informed readers know important in formation about their sources.

There are two major references for legal citation:

- Association of Legal Writing Directors & Darby Dickerson, *ALWD Citation Manual: A Professional System of Citation* (2d ed. 2003) (the *ALWD Manual*), and
- *The Bluebook: A Uniform System of Citation* (Columbia Law Review Ass'n et al. eds., 17th ed. 2000) (the *Bluebook*).

These books provide similar citation formats.

For case citations, the general rule is that the *case name* is written *as it appears* at the beginning of the opinion, *unless* it is modified by an exception—but there are many exceptions, as Rule 12 of the *ALWD Manual* and Rule 10 of the *Bluebook* explain.

Content. A case citation includes the following (where they are applicable):

- The case name, italicized and abbreviated (or not) as prescribed
- A reporter volume number
- A reporter abbreviation
- The initial page of the case
- A pinpoint page number
- Parentheses including
  —The court abbreviation
  —The date
- Subsequent history (if applicable)

Example: *Thornton v. Wahl*, 787 F.2d 1151 (7th Cir. 1986).

- **Abbreviating case names.** Legal citation format differentiates between case names in citations and case names in the text. Case names in citations have *more abbreviations.* Here is a case name in a *citation*:

    > The court later modified this rule. *Frazier v. Columbus Bd. of Educ.*, 638 N.E.2d 581 (Ohio 1994)

    Here is the same case name in *text*:

    > The court modified this rule in *Frazier v. Columbus Board of Education,* 638 N.E.2d 581 (Ohio 1994).

- **Which reporter(s) to cite.** When a case appears in more than one reporter, you must decide which reporter(s) to cite.
    - Most of the time, you should cite to **only one** reporter. Rule 12.4(a)(2) of the *ALWD Manual* and rule 10.3.1 of the *Bluebook* provide general rules for determining which reporter to use. Note that *regional reporters* are the preferred West reporter for state cases.
    - Sometimes you must cite to **all** the major reporters; this is called providing "parallel citations." *ALWD Manual* Rule 12.4(c) and *Bluebook* Rules 10.3.1 and P.3 explain the use of parallel citations.
- **Pinpoint references.** Legal citation format requires a citation to the exact page on which cited material appears. This is called a *point cite,* a *page cite,* or a *pinpoint cite.*
- **Short citations.** Use a prescribed *short citation* format after you have provided the full citation once. Note that the following is *not* a correct short citation:

    > *Jo⨯es* at 55.

    Instead, write *Jones,* 225 S.W.2d at 55.

Caution: Do **not** assume you can rely on **published citations** as models. Some sources may follow a different format, such as state citation rules; some citations have been written under outdated rules; and mistakes do occur in published sources.

Exercise 7—Format for Citations and Quotations

Correct the errors in the following citations and quotations so the items conform to either *Bluebook* or *ALWD Manual* format. Assume that each citation appears in an interoffice memorandum in the order given here and each case is mentioned in a citation (not a reference in text). If you look up a point, you may want to make a note of the page where you find it. (It is not necessary to do outside research for this exercise. If you need additional information, you may supply it or note its absence.)

1. *Dorothy Anderson, James Williams, and Sylvia M. Custer v. Superior Court* (Royal Insurance, Inc.) (App.1996) 52 Cal.Rptr.2d 792, 45 Cal.App.4th 410, stay denied, review denied.
2. *Westfield v. Ins. Exchange* (Miss. 1999), 47 So. 2d 529, rehearing denied.
3. *Batterson v. National Shoes,* 96 Cal.Rptr.2d 553, 563 (App. 2d Dist. 2000).
4. *Westfield, id.*
5. *Id at 533.*
6. *Batterson, supra.*
7. The plaintiff argued that the "Defendant had the last clear chance to avoid the accident."
8. A lawyer submitted discovery requests that were, "...boilerplate, obstructionist, frivolous, and overbroad."

Not all citation errors are equally bad. Of the first three citations above, which do you think would be the most offensive to a judge? Why?

Follow Court Rules (Chapter 8)

Guidelines

In preparing papers to be filed with a court, be sure to consult all rules and statutes that apply in your jurisdiction to the kind of document you are filing. For example, when filing papers in United States district courts, check for applicable Federal Rules of Civil Procedure, procedural statutes, local rules for your particular district, and rules for your courtroom.

Exercise 8

Assume you are preparing to file a motion for summary judgment in your local United States District Court. Check all the categories listed above and identify the applicable statutes and rules that you should consult in preparing the motion.

Do Not Plagiarize (Chapter 9)

Guidelines

Avoiding Plagiarism in Law School Papers

Some students do not adequately understand the concept of plagiarism when they enter law school. Perhaps in the past they copied material from encyclopedias or from the Internet to turn in as class reports. Some teachers may have found this copying acceptable, and others may not have checked to see whether the material was copied.

Whatever your experience in the past, it is important to understand what constitutes plagiarism at the law school level. Plagiarism can have serious consequences, including expulsion from school or ineligibility to take the bar examination.

What is plagiarism? It is *passing off someone else's words or ideas as your own.* All the following are plagiarism:

1. *Quoting language written by someone else (whether published or not) without <u>both</u> putting it in quotation marks and attributing it.* Using others' language this way implies that you wrote it, although you did not. Some apply a "five word rule," which states that when you take five words or more from another source you must put them in quotation marks and attribute them. But there are times when even fewer than five words are unique and must be attributed to their original writer.

2. *Changing a few words in language from another source and using it in your paper without quotation marks and attribution to its author.* This is still not your writing, and Rule 1 applies despite the changes.

3. *Using ideas or organization from another source without attribution.*

Why is plagiarism a serious matter? First, in the academic setting, it is important to give due credit to the person who first formulated an idea. Second, in law school your work is being evaluated in order to help you develop the ability to do competent legal work. If you turn in work that is not your own, you are not acquiring the necessary experience in legal analysis. Instead, you are being evaluated on someone else's work. If you were to receive a degree on that basis, it would be a fraud.

The legal profession has high professional standards because clients must be able to rely on lawyers for the utmost integrity. A law student who plagiarizes demonstrates a lack of fitness to accept the high trust that clients have a right to place in a lawyer.

Caution: Do not use the computer to cut-and-paste blocks of text into your notes or your document without carefully identifying the source of each block. This kind of careless copying may lead to plagiarism if you later forget the source of a quotation.

Avoiding Plagiarism in the Practice of Law

In the practice of law, plagiarism is serious for related reasons. A lawyer may use language from a form in drafting an instrument if the original writer approves the borrowing. But taking language from published sources without approval and appropriate attribution is dishonest. It is also unprofessional because it deprives the court of the lawyer's own, case-specific reasoning. And it cheats the client— the work is not tailored to the client's case, and the lawyer is asking to be paid for work that he or she did not actually do.

Some references on plagiarism

Terri LeClercq, *Failure to Teach: Due Process and Law School Plagiarism,* 49 J. Legal Educ. 236 (1999)
Eugene Volokh, *Academic Legal Writing* 209–14 (2d ed. 2005)

Exercise 9: Identifying Plagiarism

Read the original passage below. Then determine whether paragraphs A through D constitute plagiarism from it.

Original passage

Asking a lawyer for a writing sample is like asking a farmer for a manure sample: you know they've got plenty of it lying around.

> And although farmers usually aren't judged on the quality of their manure, for lawyers, the thing they have the most of—writing—is also one of the most important things they do in practice.

Mary Beth Beazley, *Getting the Legal Writing Sample You Need,* 87 Ill. B.J. 557, 557 (Oct. 1999).

Exercise

Which of the following paragraphs, if any, would constitute plagiarism from the above passage if a student submitted it as part of a paper? Assume the student does not present any more attribution than what is included here.

• Paragraph A

Asking an attorney for a writing sample is like asking a farmer for a sample of cow dung: you know they've got plenty of it around. And although farmers usually aren't judged on the quality of their cow dung, for attorneys, the thing they have the most of—writing— is also one of the most important tasks they perform in practice. Mary Beth Beazley, *Getting the Legal Writing Sample You Need,* 87 Ill. B.J. 557, 557 (Oct. 1999).

• Paragraph B

When you ask an attorney for a writing sample, it's like asking a farmer for a manure sample: they must have plenty of it around. And although farmers usually aren't judged by how good their manure is, for attorneys, writing is one of the major things they undertake in practice.

• Paragraph C

If you ask an attorney for a writing sample, you know he or she has one around somewhere. In fact, writing is the thing attorneys have the most of. Writing is one of the most important things they do.

• Paragraph D

A potential employer may appropriately ask a lawyer for a writing sample. After all, writing is a major activity for most lawyers.

Be Civil (Chapter 10)

Exercise 10A

A court dismissed a complaint that contained the following "scandalous language." Following Federal Rule of Civil Procedure 8(a), rewrite this excerpt in a more professional tone.

Green and Broberg worked closely together to keep their grandiose "Money making monster" scheme in operation... (3) by forcing the investors in various syndications to continue to make payments through the loyalty and enthusiasm of those investors who had compromised themselves to the scheme by making money by means of the Green-Broberg scheme,... Broberg aided and abetted Green in actively working to police compliance with the "pay or you are out of the deal completely" enforcement concept in this scheme that can only be described as diabolical and monstrous, by Broberg's legal advice that the forfeiture clause was legal (thus Broberg bears an awesome burden towards the investors because of his special fiduciary responsibilities as an Attorney at Law), (4) by not only failing to register this securities investment scheme to bring it under the supervision and censure of the S.E.C. but to openly operate in what was, in fact, an outlaw fashion, based on the spurious so-called "legal opinion" of Attorney Broberg, rendered to investors and potential investors, to the effect that this scheme did Not constitute securities but that, on the contrary, it was simple country-style real estate with lots of country-style profit in it for all collaborators, but destruction for the defector who will be cannibalized by the rest of the group, again based on the so-called "legal opinion" of Broberg to the effect that failure to make payments for whatever reason constitutes a breach of the so-called "trust agreement" and subjects the defector to losing his entire interest and having it assumed (cannibalized) by the remaining investors....

Gordon v. Green.

Exercise 10B

Rewrite these inflammatory statements that a lawyer included in his brief in a disciplinary proceeding against him:

> This Court should require the State of Nebraska, ex rel. Nebraska State Bar Association to pay me the sum of Five Million Dollars ($5,000,000) for the damages sustained by me and proven in the record...Anything less than $5,000,000 will do nothing but continue the three year rape that has been conducted under the color of this Court's black robes.

Nebraska ex rel. *Neb. State Bar Ass'n v. Zakrzewski.*

TABLE OF CASES CITED

Abbs v. Principi, 237 F.3d 1342 (Fed. Cir. 2001), 20

Alicia Z. v. Jose Z., 784 N.E.2d 240 (Ill. App. Ct. 2002), 43

Am. Nat'l Bank & Trust Co. of Chi. v. Harcros Chems., Inc., No. 95 C 3750, 1997 WL 413856 (N.D. Ill. July 18, 1997), 17

Anand v. Nat'l Republic Bank, No. 95 C 3940, 1996 WL 596399 (N.D. Ill. Oct. 10, 1996), 44

Anderson v. Alpha Portland Ind., Inc., 836 F.2d 1512 (8th Cir. 1988), 44

Angiulo, Commonwealth v., 615 N.E. 2d 155 (Mass. 1993), 31

Arena Land & Inv. Co. v. Petty, No. 94-4196, 1995 WL 645678 (10th Cir. Nov. 3, 1995), 30

Avery v. State Farm Mut. Auto. Ins. Co., 746 N.E.2d 1242 (Ill. App. Ct. 2001), 8, 19-20

Baird v. Pace, 752 P.2d 507 (Ariz. 1987), 5

Balthazar v. Atl. City Med. Ctr., 279 F. Supp. 2d 574 (D.N.J. 2003), 21

Banks, In re, 482 P.2d 215 (Cal. 1971), 37

Benner v. Phila. Musical Soc'y, 32 F.R.D. 197 (E.D. Pa. 1963), 29

Billing v. City of Norfolk, Va., 848 F. Supp. 630 (E.D. Va. 1994), 40

Bliss v. Rochester City Sch. Dist., 196 F. Supp. 2d 314 (W.D.N.Y. 2002), 25

Bolton, State v., 896 P.2d 830 (Ariz. 1995), 44

Borowski v. DePuy, Inc., 850 F.2d 297 (7th Cir. 1988), 9, 16

Bradshaw v. Unity Marine Corp., 147 F. Supp. 2d 668 (S.D. Tex. 2001), 8-9

Brandt v. Schal Assocs., Inc., 960 F.2d 640 (7th Cir. 1992), 28

Brehm v. Eisner, 746 A.2d 244 (Del. 2000), 25, 30

Bridges v. Robinson, 20 S.W.3d 104 (Tex. App. 2000), *disapproved on other grounds*, Telthorster v. Tennell, 92 S.W.2d 457 (Tex. 2002), 20

Bridget, State v., No. CR-318842, 1997 WL 25518 (Ohio Ct. App., Jan. 23, 1997), 37

Bridwell v. State, 507 N.E.2d 644 (Ind. Ct. App. 1987), 13

Brown v. State, 502 So. 2d 979 (Fla. Dist. Ct. App. 1987), 31, 46

Bruther v. Gen. Elec. Co., 818 F. Supp. 1238 (S.D. Ind. 1993), 4

Cal. Fin. Responsibility Co. v. Pierce, 277 Cal. Rptr. 663 (Ct. App. 1991), 39

Cannon v. Cherry Hill Toyota, 190 F.R.D. 147 (D.N.J. 1999), 54

Capitol Hardware Mfg. Co. v. Natco, Inc., 707 F. Supp. 374 (N.D. Ill. 1989), 31

Catellier v. Depco, Inc., 696 N.E.2d 75 (Ind. Ct. App. 1998), 23

Chapman v. Hootman, 999 S.W.2d 118 (Tex. App. 1999), 8

Cimino v. Yale Univ., 638 F. Supp. 952 (D. Conn. 1986), 2

Clarke v. Brandolini, No. Civ. A 90-7265, 1991 WL 16721 (E.D. Pa. Feb. 7, 1991), 17, 29

Clarke v. Brandolini, 17, 29

Clarke v. Brandolini, No. Civ. A 90-7265, 1991 WL 75185, (E.D. Pa. May 2, 1991), aff'd, 950 F.2d 721 (3d Cir. 1991) (unpublished table decision), 29

Coe, In re, 665 N.W.2d 849 (Wis. 2003), 53

Clement v. Pub. Serv. Elec. & Gas Co., 198 F.R.D. 634 (D.N.J. 2001), 6, 50

Coleman v. Thompson, 501 U.S. 722 (1991), 44

Columbus-America Discovery Group v. Atl. Mut. Ins. Co., 56 F.3d 556 (4th Cir. 1995), 41

Commonwealth v. _____ (see opposing party)

Conkling v. Turner, 18 F.3d 1285 (5th Cir. 1994), 41

Conn. Gen. Life Ins. Co. v. Chi. Title and Trust Co., 690 F.2d 115 (7th Cir. 1982), 46

Cont'l Land Co. v. Inv. Props. Co., No. M1998-00431-COA-R3-CV, 1999 WL 1129025 (Tenn. Ct. App. Dec. 10, 1999), 16

Cook v. Hilltown Township, No. CIV. A. 88-7518, 1990 WL 109985 (E.D. Pa. Aug. 1, 1990), 40

Copelco Capital, Inc., v. Gen. Consul of Bol., 940 F. Supp. 93 (S.D.N.Y. 1996), 16

Cotter v. Helmer, No. 88 Civ. 5710 (PKL), 1990 WL 103980 (S.D.N.Y. July 17, 1990), 40

David v. Village of Oak Lawn, No. 95 C 7368, 1996 WL 494268 (N.D. Ill. Aug. 27, 1996), 35

Decibus v. Woodbridge Township Police Dep't, No. Civ. A. 88-2926, 1991 WL 59428 (D.N.J. Apr. 15, 1991), 50

DeMyrick v. Guest Quarters Suite Hotels, No. 93 C 1520, 1997 WL 177838 (N.D. Ill. Apr. 6, 1997), 12

Devore v. City of Phila., No. Civ. A. 00-3598, 2004 WL 414085 (E.D. Pa. Feb. 20, 2004), 37, 79

DeWilde v. Guy Gannett Publ'g Co., 797 F. Supp. 55 (D. Me. 1992), 51

Doering v. Pontarelli Builders, Inc., No. 01 C 2924, 2001 WL 1464897 (N.D. Ill. Nov. 16, 2001), 12

Doyle v. Hasbro, Inc., 103 F.3d. 186 (1st Cir. 1996), 42

Dube, Commonwealth v., 796 N.E.2d 859 (Mass. App. Ct. 2003), 13

Eason, State v., 629 N.W.2d 625 (Wis. 2001), 28

EDC v. Navistar Int'l Transp. Corp., 915 F.2d 1082 (7th Cir. 1990), aff'd sub nom. In re EDC, Inc., 930 F.2d 1275 (7th Cir. 1991), 43

Estate of A.B., 1 Tucker 247 (N.Y. Surr. 1866), 11

Federated Mut. Ins. Co. v. Anderson, 920 P.2d 97 (Mont. 1996), 39

Fed. Intermediate Credit Bank v. Ky. Bar Ass'n, 540 S.W.2d 14 (Ky. 1976), 50

Fla. Bar v. Ray, 797 So. 2d 556 (Fla. 2001), 15

Fountain Parkway, Ltd. v. Tarrant Appraisal Dist., 920 S.W.2d 799 (Tex. Ct. App. 1996), 45

Frazier v. Columbus Bd. of Educ., 638 N.E.2d 581 (Ohio 1994), 41, 85

Frith v. State, 325 N.E.2d 186 (Ind. 1975), 51

FTC v. World Travel Vacation Brokers, Inc., 861 F.2d 1020 (7th Cir. 1988), 44

Gardner v. Investors Diversified Capital, Inc., 805 F. Supp. 874 (D. Colo. 1992), 34, 37

Generes, In re, 69 F.3d 821 (7th Cir. 1995), 33

Gershater, In re, 17 P.3d 929 (Kan. 2001), 53

Glassalum Eng'g Corp. v. 392208 Ontario Ltd., 487 So. 2d 87 (Fla. Dist. Ct. App. 1986), 2, 12

Golden Eagle Distrib. Corp. v. Burroughs Corp., 809 F.2d 584 (9th Cir.1987), 4

Golden Eagle Distrib. Corp. v. Burroughs Corp., 103 F.R.D. 124 (N.D. Cal. 1984), rev'd, 801 F.2d 1531 (9th Cir. 1986), 3-4

Gordon v. Green, 602 F.2d 743 (5th Cir. 1979), 28, 30, 91

Gosnell v. Rentokil, Inc., 175 F.R.D. 508 (N.D. Ill. 1997), 12

Gould v. Kemper Nat'l Ins. Cos., No. 93 C 7189, 1995 WL 573426 (N.D. Ill. Sept. 7, 1995), aff'd, 78 F.2d 586 (7th Cir. 1996) (unpublished table decision), 7

Great Atl. & Pac. Tea Co. v.
Town of E. Hampton, 997 F.
Supp. 340 (E.D.N.Y. 1998), 43
Green, In re Marriage of, 261
Cal. Rptr. 294 (Ct. App.
1989), 34
Greenfield v. First City Bancor-
poration of Tex., Inc., 270
B.R. 807 (N.D. Tex. 2001), 54
Griffith v. Hess Oil V.I. Corp., 5
F. Supp. 2d 336 (D.V.I. 1998),
9, 54
Guevara, In re, 41 S.W.3d 169
(Tex. App. 2001), 16
Hansen v. State Bar, 587 P.2d
1156 (Cal. 1979), 46
Hawkins, In re, 502 N.W.2d 770
(Minn. 1993), 2, 33-34, 37
Henderson v. State, 445 So. 2d
1364 (Miss. 1984), 33-34, 36
Henson v. Thezan, 717 F. Supp.
1330 (N.D. Ill. 1989), 13
Hernandez v. N.Y. Law Dep't
Corp. Counsel, No. 94 Civ.
9042 (AJP) (SS), 1997 WL
270047 (S.D.N.Y. Jan. 23,
1997) , 3, 60
Hill v. Norfolk & W. Ry., 814
F.2d 1192 (7th Cir. 1987), 20
Hi-Tek Bags, Ltd., v. Bobtron
Int'l, 144 F.R.D. 379 (C.D.
Cal. 1992), 2
Howard v. Oakland Tribune, 245
Cal. Rptr. 449 (Ct. App.
1988), 40
Huang v. Shiu, 124 F.R.D. 175
(N.D. Ill. 1988), 34
Hudson, State v., 473 S.E.2d 415
(N.C. Ct. App. 1996), rev'd on

other grounds, 483 S.E.2d 436
(N.C. 1997), 41
Hurlbert v. Gordon, 824 P.2d
1238 (Wash. Ct. App. 1992),
39
Ikari v. Mason Props., 731
N.E.2d 975 (2000), 40
Indep. Sch. Dist. No. 622 v.
Keene Corp., 511 N.W.2d 728
(Minn. 1993), 43
Iowa Supreme Court Bd. of
Prof'l Ethics and Conduct v.
Lane, 642 N.W.2d 296 (Iowa
2002), 49
Johnson v. Hunger, 266 F. Supp.
590 (S.D.N.Y. 1967), 29
Jordan v. Reis, 169 F. Supp. 2d
664 (S.D. Tex. 2001), 11
Joseph P. Caulfield & Assocs.,
Inc. v. Litho Prods., Inc., 155
F.3d 883 (7th Cir. 1998), 25
Kano v. Nat'l Consumer Co-op.
Bank, 22 F.3d 899 (9th Cir.
1994), 42
Kendall, In re Estate of, 968 P.2d
364 (Okla. Civ. App. 1998), x
Kingvision Pay Per View, Ltd. v.
Wilson, 83 F. Supp. 2d 914
(W.D. Tenn. 2000), 51
Kohler v. Woollen, Brown &
Hawkins, 304 N.E.2d 677 (Ct.
App. 1973), 46
Kouri-Perez, United States v., 8
F. Supp. 2d 133 (D.P.R. 1998),
54
Kushner v. Winterthur Swiss Ins.
Co., 620 F.2d 404 (3d Cir.
1980), 46
Ky. Bar Ass'n v. Brown, 14
S.W.3d 916 (Ky. 2000), 33

LaGrange Mem'l Hosp. v. St.
Paul Ins. Co., 740 N.E.2d 21
(Ill. App. Ct. 2000), 24

Lamore v. Ives, 977 F.2d 713 (1st
Cir. 1992), 66

Leuallen v. Borough of Paulsboro, 180 F. Supp. 2d 615
(D.N.J. 2002), 24

Lewis v. Paul Revere Life Ins.
Co., 80 F. Supp. 2d 978 (E.D.
Wis. 2000), 12, 21

Lieber v. ITT Hartford Ins. Ctr.,
Inc. 15 P.3d 1030 (Utah
2000), 7

Lockheed Martin Energy Sys.,
Inc. v. Slavin, 190 F.R.D. 449
(E.D. Tenn. 1999), 19, 54

Lord, In re Personal Restraint of,
868 P.2d 835 (Wash. 1994),
41

MacIntyre v. Butler, 181 B.R.
420 (B.A.P. 9th Cir. 1995),
aff'd, 77 F.3d 489 (9th Cir.
Feb. 14, 1996) (unpublished
table decision), 42

Maffucci v. City of Phila., No.
98-CV-2718, 1999 WL 500021
(E.D. Pa. July 15, 1999), 36

Mar, People v., 52 P.3d 95 (Cal.
2002), 13

Martin v. Hunt, 29 F.R.D. 14 (D.
Mass. 1961), 29

Massey v. Prince George's
County, 918 F. Supp. 905 (D.
Md. 1996), 10

Mass. Mut'l Life Ins. Co. v.
Aritech Corp., 882 F. Supp.
2d 190 (D. Mass. 1995), 35

McGurk v. Stenberg, 58 F. Supp.
2d 1051 (D. Neb. 1997), rev'd

on other grounds, 163 F.3d 470
(8th Cir. 1998), 6

McHenry v. Renne, 84 F.3d 1172
(9th Cir. 1996), 30

McNeel v. Pub. Serv. Co., 923 F.
Supp. 1316 (D. Colo. 1996),
40

Mendez v. Draham, 182 F. Supp.
2d 430 (D.N.J. 2002), 24

Merrill v. Cintas Corp., 941 F.
Supp. 1040 (D.C. Kan. 1996),
46

Mitchell v. Holly Sugar Corp.,
No. 301940, 2003 WL
1880155 (Cal. Ct. App. Apr.
16, 2003), 44

Molina-Tarazon, United States v.,
285 F.3d 807 (9th Cir. 2002),
30

Moore v. Regents of the Univ. of
Cal., 793 P.2d 479 (Cal.
1990), 50

Morgan v. South Bend Cmty.
Sch. Corp., 797 F.2d 471 (7th
Cir. 1986), 41

Morgens Waterfall Holdings,
L.L.C., v. Donaldson, Lufkin
& Jenrette Sec. Corp., 198
F.R.D. 608 (S.D.N.Y. 2001),
30

Morters v. Barr, No. 01-2011,
2003 WL 115359 (Wis. Ct.
App. Jan. 14, 2003), 19

Nebraska ex rel. Neb. State Bar
Ass'n v. Zakrzewski, 560
N.W.2d 150 (Neb. 1997), 15,
92

Nguyen v. IBP, Inc., 162 F.R.D.
675 (D. Kan. 1995), 15

Nolan, *In re*, 706 N.Y.S.2d 704 (N.Y. App. Div. 2000), 15

Northwestern Nat'l Ins. Co. v. Guthrie, No. 90 C 04050, 1990 WL 205945 (N.D. Ill. Dec. 3, 1990), 1

Novartis Consumer Health Inc., v. Elan Transdermal Technologies, Inc., 209 F.R.D. 507 (2002), 42

N/S Corp. v. Liberty Mut. Ins. Co., 127 F.3d 1145 (9th Cir. 1997), ix, 6, 15, 16

Olander v. French, 680 N.E.2d 962 (Ohio 1997), 44

Pagan Velez v. Laboy Alvarado, 145 F. Supp. 2d 146 (D.P.R. 2001), 51

People v. _____ (see opposing party)

Phila. Gear Corp. v. Swath Int'l, Ltd., 200 F. Supp. 2d 493 (E.D. Pa. 2002), 55

Philips v. United States, No. 95-1404, 1996 WL 43621 (E. D. La. Feb. 3, 1997), 46

Pickens v. State, 105 S.W.3d 746 (2003), 45

Pierotti v. Torian, 96 Cal. Rptr. 2d 553 (Ct. App. 2000), 10, 39

Pinotti, *In re* Disciplinary Action Against, 585 N.W.2d 55 (Minn. 1998), 28

P.M.F. Servs., Inc. v. Grady, 681 F. Supp. 549 (N.D. Ill. 1988), 37

Politico v. Promus Hotels, Inc., 184 F.R.D. 232 (E.D.N.Y. 1999), 30, 50

Precision Specialty Metals, Inc., v. United States, 315 F.3d 1346 (Fed. Cir. 2003), 3

Prickett v. DeKalb County, 92 F. Supp. 2d 1357 (N.D. Ga. 2000), 11

Prop. Movers, L.L.C., v. Goodwin, 31 Fed. Appx. 81 (4th Cir. 2002), 20

Qualls v. Apfel, 206 F.3d 1368 (10th Cir. 2000), 15

Quirk v. Premium Homes, Inc., 999 S.W.2d 306 (Mo. Ct. App.1999), x

Ramseur v. Barreto, 216 F.R.D. 180 (D.D.C. 2003), 45

Randall v. Salvation Army, 686 P.2d 241 (Nev. 1984), 13

Ray v. Chisum, 260 S.W.2d 118 (Tex. Civ. App. 1953), x

Responsibility Co. v. Pierce, 277 Cal. Rptr. 663 (Ct. App. 1991), 39

Richards, *In re*, 755 N.E.2d 601 (Ind. 2001), 15

Rodriguez v. Chen, No. CV 95-130-TUC-RMB, 1996 WL 159810 (D. Ariz. Feb. 7, 1996), 40

Roeder v. Islamic Republic of Iran, 195 F. Supp. 2d 140 (D.D.C. 2002), 8

Romala Corp. v. United States, 927 F.2d 1219 (Fed. Cir. 1991), 20

Rubino v. Circuit City Stores, Inc., 758 N.E.2d 1 (Ill. Ct. App. 2001), 24

Salahuddin v. Coughlin, 999 F. Supp. 526 (S.D.N.Y. 1998), 12

Sampson, United States *ex rel.*, v. Crescent City E.M.S., Inc., No. Civ. A. 96-3505, 1997 WL 570688 (E.D. La. Sept. 12, 1997), 19

Schutts v. Bently Nev. Corp., 966 F. Supp. 1549 (D. Nev. 1997), 6

Sidwell Constr. Co. v. Dist. 837 Aeorspace Workers Credit Union, 660 S.W.2d 753 (Mo. Ct. App. 1983), 45

Shepperson, *In re*, 674 A.2d 1273 (Vt. 1996), 2, 39

S Indus., Inc. v. JL Audio, Inc., 29 F. Supp. 2d 878 (N.D. Ill. 1998), 42

Slater v. Gallman, 339 N.E.2d 863 (N.Y. 1975), 28-29

Smith v. Lewis, 530 P.2d 589 (Cal. 1975), *overruled on other grounds, In re* Marriage of Brown, 544 P.2d 561 (Cal. 1976), 4-5

Smith v. United Transp. Union Local No. 81, 594 F. Supp. 96 (S.D. Cal. 1984), 3

Southern N. H. Water Co. v. Town of Hudson, 649 A.2d 847 (N.H. 1994), 43

Staffilino Chevrolet, Inc. v. Ohio Motor Vehicle Dealers Bd., 635 N.E.2d 41 (Ohio 1994), 41

State v. _____ (see opposing party)

Sterling v. Alexander, 99 S.W.3d 793 (Tex. App. 2003), 20

Stevens v. O'Neill, 62 N.E. 424 (N.Y. 1902), 27

Stone, *In re*, 672 A.2d 1032 (D.C. Ct. App. 1995), 34

Stone v. House of Day Funeral Serv., Inc., 748 N.E.2d 1200 (Ohio Ct. App. 2000), 16

Stork, People v., 713 N.E.2d 187 (Ill. App. Ct. 1999), 21

St. Paul Reinsurance Co., Ltd. v. Commercial Fin. Corp., 198 F.R.D. 508 (N.D. Iowa 2000), 53, 55, 68

Styles v. Phila. Elec. Co., No. CIV. A. 93-4593, 1994 WL 245469 (E.D. Pa. June 6, 1994), 34

Swallow, State v., 405 N.W.2d 29 (S.D. 1987), 31

Taylor v. Belger Cartage Serv., Inc., 102 F.R.D. 172 (W.D. Mo. 1984), 5

Taylor v. Lenawee County Bd. of Road Comm'rs, 549 N.W.2d 80 (Mich. Ct. App. 1996), 45

Taylor, United States v., 258 F.3d 815 (8th Cir. 2001), 25

Teague v. Bakker, 213 F. Supp. 2d 571 (W.D.N.C. 2002), 37

Teamsters Local No. 579 v. B & M Transit, Inc., 882 F.2d 274 (7th Cir. 1989), 3

Thomas & Betts Corp. v. Panduit Corp., No. 93 C 4017, 1996 WL 169396 (N.D. Ill. April 9, 1996), 44

Thomas v. Thomas, 661 N.W.2d 1 (S.D. 2003), 44, 54

Thomason v. Norman E. Lehrer, P.C., 182 F.R.D. 121 (D.N.J. 1998), *aff'd*, 189 F.3d 465 (3d

Cir.1999) (unpublished table decision), 54

Thornton v. Wahl, 787 F.2d 1151 (7th Cir. 1986), 1, 3, 84

TK-7 Corp. v. Estate of Barbouti, 966 F.2d 578 (10th Cir. 1992), 43

Trapp v. Schuyler Constr., 197 Cal. Rptr. 411 (Ct. App. 1983), 35, 79

Trust Co. v. N.N.P., Inc., 104 F.3d 1478, 1485 (5th Cir. 1997), 44

Tyler v. State, 47 P.3d 1095 (Alaska Ct. App. 2001), 10, 16

United States v._____ (see opposing party)

USA Clio Biz, Inc., v. N.Y. State Dep't of Labor, No. 97 CV ·250, 1998 WL 57176 (E.D.N.Y. Jan. 3, 1998), 50

Vandeventer v. Wabash Nat'l Corp., 893 F. Supp. 827 (N.D. Ind. 1995), 47

Varda, Inc. v. Ins. Co. of N. Am., 45 F.3d 634 (2d Cir. 1995), 42

Vasquez, People v., 520 N.Y.S.2d 99 (N.Y. Crim. Ct. 1987), 36

Walden, State v., 905 P.2d 974 (Ariz. 1995), 42

Walder v. State, 85 S.W.3d 824 (Tex. App. 2002), 8

Wallace Computers Servs., Inc., v. David Noyes & Co., No. 93 C 6005, 1994 WL 75201 (N.D. Ill., March 9, 1994), 7

Weissman v. Fruchtman, No. 83 Civ. 8958 (PKL), 1986 WL 15669 (S.D.N.Y. Oct. 31, 1986), 40

Wells Fargo Bank v. Marshall, 24 Cal. Rptr. 2d 507 (App. 1993), 37

Westinghouse Elec. Corp. v. NLRB, 809 F.2d 419 (7th Cir. 1987), 42

Wilkins, In re, 782 N.E.2d 985 (Ind. 2002), 53

Yankee Candle Co. v. Bridgewater Candle Co., 140 F. Supp. 2d 111 (D. Mass. 2001), aff'd, 259 F.3d 25 (1st Cir. 2001), 28

Young v. City of Palm Bay, 358 F.3d 859 (11th Cir. 2004), 45

Index

abuse of process, 5, 6
ad hominem arguments, *see* personal attacks
adverse authority, *see* authority, contrary
advocacy
  effective, 42
  tactics, 1, 5
  vigorous, duty of, 3, 4
affidavit, 36
  false, 15
  misleading,16
  use to circumvent page limit, 43
agreements, *see* contracts
ALWD Citation Manual, 84, 85, 86
amended complaint, *see* complaint
amend, leave to, 17, 29
analysis, 50, 51
  good, 13
  faulty, 11, 19–21
  lack of, 6
and/or, use of, 25
annotated code, 6
apology, order to write, 54
apostrophe, misuse of, 34, 36, 37

appendix, use of to circumvent page limit, 42
applying law to facts, lack of, 19
arguments,
  ad hominem, *see* personal attacks
  baseless, 19
  frivolous, *see* frivolous
  illogical, 20
  irrelevant, 20, 21, 23, 29
  orderly, 23
  undeveloped, 21, 25
article, order to write, 55
attorney's fees, 3, 4, 6, 7, 9, 10, 16, 19, 23, 28, 37, 39, 45, 51
authority,
  contrary, omission of, ix, 3, 4, 8, 9, 10, 11, 12
  controlling, omission of, 2, 6, 11, 12
  inadequate, 9–10
  irrelevant, 20
  relevant, omission of, 2, 9–10, 10–11, 13
bad faith, 10
bankruptcy
  course, 2

bankruptcy *continued*
    court rules, 2
bar discipline, *see* disciplinary
    action
baseless claim, *see* frivolous
Berring, Robert C., 59
Bluebook, 40, 84, 85, 86
blunderbuss, 25, 54
boilerplate objections, 55, 67
brief,
    page limit, see separate entry
        page limit
    stricken, 16, 43
    succinct, 27
    well-written, x, 13, 31
    word limit, see separate entry
        word limit
candor, duty of, 3, 51
capital case, 44
cases, *see* authority
chutzpah, 54
citations,
    erroneous, 9, 37, 39–40
    failure to provide, 8, 39
    record, 10
    pinpoint, 9, 23, 40
    short guide, 84
    subsequent history, 40
citation form, order to obtain tu-
    toring in, 39
civil rights claim, 6
civility, 53–55, 91
clarity, x, 23
    lack of, 11, 16, 23, 24, 25, 29,
        33, 49
clauses, 25
client, order to send court's
    opinion to, 24
client, sanctions against, *see*
    sanctions

comma, 35, 36, 80–82
community property interest, 4, 5
competence, duty of, 1, 6, 11
complaint, 6, 19, 24, 49
    amended, 29, 30, 45, 55
    from form book, 50
computer research, 7, 11
computers, 27; *see also* mouse
    clicks, spacing, typeface,
    Westlaw, word processing
conciseness, 24, 27, 30, 31; *see*
    also wordiness and ver-
    bosity
concise statement of factual dis-
    agreements, *see* statement
    of undisputed facts
contempt, citation for, 2
contracts, 49
    statute of limitations, 21
controlling authority, *see* author-
    ity
copies, failure to file, 46
copyright issue, 51
correction fluid, 11
costs,
    denial of motion for, 42
    order to pay, 3, 9, 10, 16, 19,
        20, 23, 24, 28, 29, 39, 49
counsel, ineffective assistance of,
    6
course, order to take,
    bankruptcy, 2
    civil procedure, 16
    citation form, 39
    civil rights, 6
    federal practice, 6, 21, 24, 47
    legal writing, 2, 34
    professionalism, 24
    professional responsibility, 21
    Rule 11, 47

court
  admonishment by, 15, 24, 50,
    53
  burden on, ix, 6, 7–8, 8, 15,
    17, 28, 40, 44, 45, 46
  commendation by, x, 13, 31,
    47
  negative comment by, 3, 4, 7,
    11, 12, 17, 25, 28, 29, 30,
    31, 34, 35, 36, 37, 38, 40,
    41, 43, 45
  reprimand, 54
  reproach by, 3, 13, 20, 21
  warning by, 4, 20, 46, 47
  courtesy, x, 36, 55; see also civil-
    ity
court rules
  exercise, 87
  violation of, 23, 34, 41–47
credibility, x
criminal case, 6, 37
cross-references, confusing, 29
cut-and-paste word processing,
  24
deadlines, see timeliness
deed, inaccurate, 16
depublished case, 6
Dickerson, Darby, 84
dictionaries, legal, 60
direct expression, 64
disbarment, 15
disciplinary action, x, 9, 15, 23,
  39, 46, 49, 51
  for incompetence, 23
  suspension from practice, 2,
    13, 23, 28, 33, 34, 47, 49
  order to inform State Bar of
    court's opinion, 10
dismiss, motion to, 16
dismissal of

appeal, 16, 23, 44, 45, 46
case, 6, 13, 29, 30, 46
claims, 2, 21, 34
complaint, 6, 33, 50
dismissed claims, resubmitting,
  19, 21, 29, 55
dissenting opinion, citation to,
  20
District of Columbia Court of
  Appeals, 34
divorce case, 4–5
drunk driving, 6
Dunn, Donald J., 59
duty to know the law, see law
Dylan, Bob, citation to, 13
Edinger, Elizabeth A., 59
editing,
  at last minute, 45
  lack of, 23
  order requiring, 29, 30
Eighth Circuit, 6, 24
elegance, 31
Elizabethan England, ix
ellipses, misleading, 17
Enquist, Anne, 76, 77, 83
ethics, x, 1, 10
excusable neglect, 45
exercises,
  apostrophe, 83
  citations, 86
  civility, 91, 92
  clarity, 65
  comma, 81
  court rules, 87
  grammar, 77
  legalese, 65, 66, 69
  plagiarism, 89
  proofreading, 77, 79
  providing cogent analysis, 62
  spelling, 77, 79

exercises *continued*
  stating the law accurately,
    59–60
  wordiness, 65, 66, 67, 69
extension of existing law, argu-
    ment for, 4
facts, generally, 15–17
  misstatement of, 15
  misrepresenting, ix, 15, 16
  omission of, 11, 20
  presentation as argument, 20
fallacies, 61–62
false premises, 20
Federal Express, filing by, 45
federal practice and procedure,
    6, 21
fees, 8; *see also* attorney's fees
footnotes, use of to circumvent
    page limit, 42–44
forensic embroidery, 30
form books, 6, 30, 49, 50
forthwith, 3
frivolous
  appeal, 20
  argument, 3
  claim, 1, 8, 19, 28, 29, 47
  complaint, 24
  document, ix, 6
  objections, 55
Garner, Bryan, A., 28, 60, 65
gibberish, 30
gobbledygook, 30; *see also*
    wordiness and verbosity;
    clarity; legalese
google.com, reliance on,13
grammar
  errors, 23, 33, 34, 37
  guidelines, 75
  references on, 76
  subject-verb agreement, 34

guidelines,
  apostrophe, 82
  citations, 84
  clarity, 64
  court rules, 87
  grammar, 75
  legalese, 64
  plagiarism, 88
  proofreading, 77
  providing cogent analysis, 61
  punctuation, 80
  stating the facts accurately, 60
  stating the law accurately, 57
  spelling, 77
  wordiness, 64
habeas corpus, 6
Hacker, Diana, 76, 83
hearsay, 36
Horner, Winifred Bryan, 76, 83
hostages in Iran, 8
indictment, 34, 36
ineffectiveness of counsel, 6, 37
information, disclosure of pro-
    tected, 2
instruments, 49, 50
investigation of facts, inade-
    quate, 16
Kent, Samuel B., Judge, 9
late filing, *see* timeliness
law,
  duty to discover, 5
  duty to know, 5, 11
  misrepresenting, x, 2, 3, 4, 24
  misstating, generally, 1–12
    intentional, 2, 3
    reckless, 2, 3
  outdated, 7
  sloppy statement of, 3
  stating accurately, 1
  unsettled, 4–5

LeClercq, Terri, 49, 65, 83, 89
legal encyclopedia, citation to, 13
legalese, 25, 27, 28, 64
legal writing
  course, 2
  good, x, 31
letter, discourteous, 53
limitations period, *see* statute of
  limitations
literate bar, 34
list of similar cases, order to file,
  11
logic, poor, 19–21, 25, 28, 34
malpractice, 4, 5, 11, 45–46
Marks, Thomas C., 62
Mersky, Roy M., 59
metaphor, 20
minimalist analytic wizardry, 9
misrepresenting facts, *see* facts
misrepresenting the law, *see* law
misstating the law, *see* law
modification of existing law, argument for, 4
mouse clicks, 24
New Testament, citation to, 13
New York Court of Appeals, 29
Ninth Circuit, 4, 16, 42
non sequiturs, 20
notice of appeal, tardy, 44, 45\
nouns, clumsy, 65
Oates, Laurel Currie, 76, 83
obfuscation, *see* clarity, lack of
obstructionist tactics, 55
opposing authority, *see* contrary
  authority
opposing party, burden on, 20,
  28, 39, 45
organization, 20
orthography, 37
ostrich, behaving like, 8, 9

overruled case, 1, 7, 12, 13, 24
p's and q's, judge's counsel to
  watch, 12
page limit, 23, 24, 41–44, 47
  affidavit used to evade, 43
  excuse for omitting relevant
    material, 44
  citation to other briefs to cir-
    cumvent limit, 43
  footnotes used to evade,
    42–44
  motions crafted to evade, 42
  renumbering to evade, 43
  use of combined brief to cir-
    cumvent limit, 44
paragraph, long, 30
passive voice, defined, 64–65
period, 36
personal attacks, 19, 23, 54
pinpoint citations, *see* citations
plain English, 27
plain meaning of statute, *see*
  statute
plagiarism, 49–51
  guidelines, 88–89
  in law school, 49, 88
  in practice, 49–50, 89
plea agreement, 24
Posner, Judge, 20, 46
possessive case, 36
Pound, Roscoe, 53
precision, x
prejudice, 6, 30
Prince George's County, 11
professionalism, x, 16, 39, 46, 55
professional standards, ix
prolix, *see* wordiness and verbosity
proofreading, 37, 77–79
prospectus, fabricated, 15

public, harm to, 20, 33
public reprimand, *see* reprimand
punctuation, 35–38, 80–83; *see
    also* apostrophe, comma,
    period
quotations,
    altering, 3
    format for, 86
    long, 19
    selective and misleading, 16
Raimes, Ann, 76, 83
'Rambo' tactics, 53, 55, 67; *see
    also* obstructionist tactics
record,
    failure to review, 18
    misstatement of, 15, 16, 17
redundant, 30
reprimand, 6
    formal, 3
    public, 2, 13, 34, 37
reproach by court, *see* court
research,
    competent, 1, 13
    guidelines, 57
    inadequate, 4, 5, 6, 7, 24
    plan, 57
    sloppy, 1
    standard techniques, 5
restrictive modifiers, 35–36
revising, 77
Root, Elihu, 5
Rule 11, 3, 6, 7, 19, 28, 33, 47
    order to write about, 24
rules, court, *see* court rules
sanctions, 2, 3, 6, 7, 9, 10, 16,
    19, 20, 23, 24, 28, 29, 39,
    41, 42, 46, 47, 54
    against client, 9, 20
    motion for, 2, 28

order to show cause re, 3, 7,
    12, 18, 34, 42, 50
order to reveal to other
    courts, 19
payable to court, 10
reduced fee, 38
security interest, perfecting, 5
sentence, lengthy, 30, 65
settlement offer, 36
Seventh Circuit, 2, 3, 9, 25, 28,
    42
Shakespeare, 33, 34
Shapo, Helene, 62
Shapo, Marshall, 62
shepardize, 3, 5, 12
Shepard's, 1
    'questioned' notation, 12
    'overruled' notation, 12
sic, 35, 37, 38, 79
spacing, 42, 43, 44
spelling errors, 33, 34, 35, 37,
    38, 79
standard of review, 8
statement of the case, 23
statement of undisputed facts,
    28, 42
statute of limitations, 21, 45
statute, plain meaning of, 20
stenography, 27
stricken,
    brief, 43
    motions, 42
Strunk , William, 30, 65
student comment, reliance on,
    13
succinctness, 27; *see also* wordi-
    ness and verbosity
summary judgment, 20
    motion for, 4, 11, 28, 42

superior,
    order to file affidavit of, 12
    order to bring to court, 3
suspension from practice, *see*
    disciplinary action
syntax, *see* grammatical errors
tactical decisions, 5
taxes, waste of, 20
Third Circuit, 46
timeliness, 44–46
torts, statute of limitations, 21
treatise, copying from, 49, 51
trust, 37
typeface, 23, 42, 43, 44, 47
typographical errors, x, 33, 36,
    37, 39
unclear writing, *see* clarity
unfounded claim, *see* frivolous
update authority, failure to, 1,
    11, 12
verbosity, *see* wordiness
Volokh, Eugene, 89
waiver of arguments, 20
Walker, Timothy, 27

warning by court, *see* court
Webster, Daniel, 23
Westlaw
    misreading, 7
    natural language search, 11
White, E.B., 30, 65
will, fabricated, 15
wordiness, ix, x, 25, 27–31, 43
    guuidelines for eliminating,
        64
word limits, 41, 44
    excuse for omitting argu-
        ments, 44
word processing, 24, 28, 43, 44
    cut-and-paste, 24
    mouse clicks, 24
    spacing, *see* spacing
    temptations toward wordi-
        ness, 28
    typeface, *see* typeface
writing style, ix, x, 13; *see also*
    legal writing
Wydick, Richard C., 65